W.H. Davies

In Memory of Gareth

W.H. DAVIES

Lawrence Normand

Border Lines Series Editor
John Powell Ward

seren

Seren is the book imprint of
Poetry Wales Press Ltd
Nolton Street, Bridgend, Wales
www.seren-books.com

© Lawrence Normand, 2003
Editorial and Afterword © John Powell Ward, 2003
First published in 2003

ISBN 1-85411-260-0 hbk
ISBN 1-85411-261-9 pbk
A CIP record for this title is available from
the British Library

The publisher works with the financial assistance
of the Welsh Books Council

Front Cover: Davies photographed for his volume, *Beggars*, 1909

Printed in Palatino by Cromwell Press, Wiltshire

Contents

List of Illustrations

One: Family and Early Years 1871-1893

W.H. Davies was born in 1871 in Newport, Monmouthshire, Wales and, according to John Press writing in 1981, was 'English'. In 1920 Harold Munro, the publisher of the Georgian Poetry volumes, wrote of Davies, 'He is typically English'. These comments suggest that although Davies was a Welshman, born and educated in Newport, his writing is imaginatively English. Davies's life followed a remarkable route from an obscure working-class childhood in Wales to middle-class security in a Gloucestershire village, and some fame, in Britain and the English-speaking world, as a poet; and this might suggest a simple shift from Welsh origins to English identity. But this journey was not simple or straightforward, and involved more indirections than the simple crossing from Wales to England, in geographical and cultural terms, would imply. Davies's self-creation as a writer began in his adolescence and eventually involved almost every aspect of his complex past.

The Davies family history was part of the history of Newport. During the nineteenth century Newport was expanding rapidly and drawing in immigrants from north and west Wales, from England, especially the areas round the Severn estuary, as well as Ireland, Italy, and other parts of Europe. In 1801 its population was 1,400, by 1861 it stood at 25,000, and it continued to grow dramatically until around 1921. By the mid-nineteenth century Newport was a fast-growing port for the booming coal and iron industries of the south Wales valleys. One side of Davies's family were English immigrants from Cornwall. His grandfather, Captain Francis Boase Davies, was a master mariner who settled in Newport to become landlord of the Church House Inn in Portland Street. Davies's paternal grandmother came from Somerset. The maternal side of the family was Welsh: Davies's mother, Mary Ann Davies, was the daughter of a shoemaker called Gomer Evans whose family lived in Abersychan, a village near Pontypool. Davies's family connections spread out into both Wales and England, and like many people in south-east Wales in the nineteenth century he would have family memories and cultural familiarity with both sides of the border.

The Welsh-speaking part of that culture had virtually disappeared in Monmouthshire by the 1870s. Even in 1854 George Borrow reckoned that only about half the people in rural east Monmouthshire spoke Welsh. From the mid-nineteenth century the industrial south-east, including the towns along the heads of the valleys and the ports of Swansea, Cardiff and Barry, attracted huge numbers of workers from other parts of Wales and beyond, many displaced from working on the land. There was a massive shift of the Welsh population so that by the end of the century the industrial south contained, according to Gwyn Williams, around two-thirds to three-quarters of the Welsh population, and had become 'an export metropolis of a world economy ... merging inexorably into an overarching culture of the world language of English' (*WWW* 181). Davies grew up in the midst of this social, economic and industrial transformation. The house where he lived with his grandparents was less than a hundred yards from the old town dock where he could see the masts and rigging of the tall ships. By 1888, when Davies was seventeen, Newport was the sixth busiest port in Britain, on a par with Glasgow, and its ships sailed worldwide. To Davies it must have offered chances for travel and experience in the world, even if he had not already had his sense of seagoing sharpened by his grandfather's personal experience. As part of the British imperial economy, its dominant culture was English. When in the mid-1890s the Welsh home rule movement that was finding support in mid and north Wales sought support in the anglicised cities of the south, it was spurned. At a public meeting in Newport one speaker roundly declared that south-east Wales rejected 'the domination of Welsh ideas' (*WWW* 230-1).

Although Newport was part of the south's dynamic industrial belt, the suburb of Pillgwenlly where William Davies was born was not far from the countryside bordering the town. As a boy Davies would walk to Tredegar Park through which the Ebbw river flowed and where a deer herd was kept. His boyhood and upbringing might have followed a familiar pattern of working-class life, with emphasis on the nuclear family and home, a work ethic, and non-conformist respectability, had it not been for two events that fractured Davies's family, and led to an unusual upbringing.

Davies was born on 20 April 1871 at 14 Portland Street, Newport. He was the second son of Francis Davies, an iron-moulder, and Mary Ann Davies. The first son, Francis, was simple-minded. In 1873 a sister, Matilda, was born, but in the same year the father of the family died at the age of thirty-one, leaving his widow to cope with three children under five. Mary Davies received money from her father-in-law to support herself and her children, but when she took the sensible step that would guarantee her own and her children's security by remarrying, she found herself at odds with her father-in-law. Captain Davies refused her any more money and offered instead that he and his wife should adopt the three children provided that Mary Davies give up all claim to them, which she agreed to do. The children suffered a double loss: the death of their father was followed by the effective loss of their mother; and their sense of the unconditional security of home and family love must have been destroyed by these deeply unsettling events. Mary Davies remarried to become Mrs Joseph Hill, and continued to live in Newport, raising a second family in which the children of her first husband had no part. In 1875 Davies's grandparents adopted the three children, who moved to the Church House Inn, a few doors along Portland Street from the house where they were born.

When Davies was sixty and remembering his childhood, he said, 'My mother married again and left us when we were small'. His interlocutor, Brian Waters, thought that his words were chosen carefully and expressed the fact that he had never forgiven his mother (BC 15). Waters attributed Davies's distrust of emotional closeness to others to this trauma, conjecturing that 'the far-reaching result of this experience was that he never allowed anyone to hurt him again, and gave his heart to no one'. Waters thinks that it was his mother's remarriage that shaped Davies's emotional and sexual relations with women, and this is very likely true, though there's misogyny in Waters' comment that Davies was 'a realist in his relationships with women, about whom he had no illusions'. Davies's sexual life depended on casual encounters and short-term attachments with women until he married at the age of fifty-two. His poetry shows no misogyny or cynicism towards women, and it dwells mostly on the pleasures of sexual desire and love-making, even in the period after his marriage. But it does not explore the unfolding of emotional or sexual love, its intricacy or intensity, from the point of view of someone inside a long-term relationship, and to this extent Waters is right in pinpointing emotional defensiveness as a central feature of Davies's personality. But Davies's childhood loss involved not just his mother's remarriage but also his father's death. His emotional distrust may have extended to relations with men as well as women, and indeed close male friendships are relatively rare in Davies's life or in his writing.

Church House public house contained two quite different influences on Davies in his grandfather and grandmother, for Captain Davies was a sociable, drinking man, as befitted a publican, and Lydia Davies was a staunch member of the Commercial Road Baptist Chapel. Mary Davies, Davies's mother, was illiterate until the age of forty, when remarkably she turned herself into an enthusiastic reader. Davies himself did not go to primary school until he was eight and the family moved to 38 Raglan Street on Captain Davies's retirement, perhaps, according to Sybil Hollingdrake, because his grandmother objected to his attending a local Anglican school. Lydia Davies represented a narrow, Welsh nonconformist morality. Davies told the story of his grandmother's smacking him for some disobedience, and saying between blows that if he carried on like that he would be 'no better than that young Brobribb cousin of yours, who's brought disgrace upon the family!' This referred to a Somerset relation of hers, the famous actor Henry Irving. For Lydia Davies the stage was always 'the devil's playground'. Nevertheless, she was committed to education in a way that Davies's illiterate mother might not have been.

Davies's grandfather offered the boy a very different model from the puritanical grandmother. His memories were of a life at sea. He would pace up and down the passage of his house as if he were still at sea, and when the house was locked up for the night he would ask, 'Is everything made fast?' The old man's public house no doubt had sailors among its customers. The poem 'The Call of the Sea' (*FP*) registers the indelible memories that sailors have of the sea, 'old sea-faring men that fear / Land more than water', and who 'hear again / Men's voices in a hurricane'. Captain Davies loved to drink, as his grandson would do, and it is possible, as happens to many publicans, that he gave up his publican's licence because of his excessive drinking. He would give his grandchildren beer to drink before they went to bed. However, in the harshness of his judgements Captain Davies was perhaps similar to his wife, for he required his daughter-in-law to have no more to do with her children when they were adopted. And, in 'The Child and the Mariner' (*SJ*) the judgement passed on the mariner who mesmerised children with his exotic stories is also severe: '"A damn bad sailor and a landshark too, / No good in port or out" – my granddad said'.

Davies went first to Temple Street Boys' School in 1879 where the headmaster, William Richards, provided not only the standard curriculum in reading, writing and arithmetic, but also demonstrated his own enthusiasm for literature by reciting such poems as Campbell's 'Battle of the Baltic' as well as the poems that appeared in the classroom textbooks, the series known as 'The Royal Readers'. Lawrence Hockey's research has uncovered details of the education that William Davies would have received at Temple Street School, and later Alexandra Road Boys' School which he attended from 1883 to 1885. Teachers had to provide the three basic subjects, but headmasters could also teach singing, English, geography, or history and thereby receive extra grant. The reading syllabus was designed to direct the boys step by step towards the canonical writers of English prose and poetry. The model of culture provided for Davies and other boys was English literary culture with the authoritative stamp of 'greatness' it was supposed to bear, and which made it the appropriate expression of an imperial power. South Wales, of course, played a major part in the British empire's world economic dominance. Its coal was exported world-wide, and its capital ventures and entrepreneurship extended to north and south America, Europe and Russia. The cultural capital of the empire, which was exported along with its coal and other products, had canonical English literature as one of its main components. Boys in working-class Newport were inducted into its mysteries along with those in England, the West Indies, the United States, and anywhere else British influence extended. But the influence of English literature did not go unchallenged in Davies's education. The headmaster of Alexandra Road Boys' School, Richard Lewis, asserted the existence of Welsh-language literature. Lewis was the author of *Cambrian Lyrics*, a collection of famous Welsh lyrics in English translation, meant for use in schools. As well as demonstrating the intricate metrical patterns of much Welsh poetry – and thereby imparting metrical knowledge useful for a future writer – this collection would remind the boys that until the nineteenth century most of the poetry of Monmouthshire was written in Welsh. At school then Davies learned something of the variety of metrical forms possible in Welsh and English.

Both Davies's headmasters were markedly Christian. Temple Street School was a church school where there was a good deal of scripture teaching, including memorising passages of the bible. This part of his education left its mark on Davies's writing, in its echoing of biblical language, as well as its absorption of broad, Christian ethical principles. When Davies was a tramp in England he always carried a Bible with him. The headmaster of Alexandra Road School was a prominent member of Davies's grandmother's Baptist Chapel, and it may have been his presence that made Davies's grandmother send the boy there rather than a school nearer their home. Baptist or Christian ways of life were rejected by Davies as an adolescent and in later life, but the education he received at his schools clearly shaped his mind and imagination. His headmasters' passion for the written word, either as scripture or literature, encouraged a similar passion in him. The rhythms and words of the bible sound through his poetry and prose. Phrases from his school reading books, sometimes word for word, have been traced in his writing by Hockey, suggesting that Davies had a strongly verbal imagination and a verbal memory.

William Davies's name first appeared in print, however, not as an author but as a petty thief. If the pillars of respectable working-class life consisted of obeying the law, finding pride in work, and observing rules of sexual propriety, then Davies was eventually to violate all these codes. He began as a boy of thirteen by turning delinquent. At Alexandra Road Boys' School he joined a shoplifting gang that stole from local shops and he and another boy were caught in the act of stealing two bottles of scent. Five boys were taken to court by three shopkeepers, and each was sentenced to several strokes of the birch, the number depending on the severity of the offence. The boys found guilty of stealing handbags were the most severely punished, one boy receiving twenty-four strokes, two boys eighteen, Davies receiving twelve strokes, and another six. Captain Davies reportedly offered to pay a fine of thirty pounds to allow his grandson to avoid the birch. A report of the case appeared in the *Monmouthshire Merlin* on 25 January 1884. This incident, when it was retold in the *Autobiography of a Super-Tramp*, was slightly changed to reflect greater glory on Davies who there became the leader of the gang, and one of the two boys receiving most strokes of the birch. Davies is happy to change the details of this and other stories if it produces a more flattering self-image or a better story. None of his autobiographical writings should be taken as accurate accounts of what actually happened (though often they are the only accounts we have).

The boy's petty thievery caused shame and disappointment in Davies's grandparents, who confined him to the immediate vicinity of the house. Davies later represented himself shedding 'real tears of repentance' when his schoolmaster admonished him. But this incident must also have given him a reputation for daring and toughness among other local boys and girls. And this is the aspect of the story he is keen for his later readers to recognise too. As an adolescent constructing an identity for himself he shows, perhaps inadvertently, several conflicting aspects of a developing self that has risked and survived a defiance of the law: contrition at the transgression, but also pride in coming through it well. The adult Davies would put himself outside the law, or on its boundaries, when he was a tramp in the USA and England, and for much the same reasons as the boy, in order to fashion a satisfying identity for desires that were divergent and difficult to reconcile to conventional social life. He chose to live, at certain periods of his life, among degraded, violent men; and yet his writing was to depend on his sensitive responses to the natural and human world. It may be that the intensely masculine aspect of his personality, and the risks and challenges that he faced it with, was a shield for his sensitivity, even indeed vulnerability, and the condition that allowed it to be expressed. Certainly as a boy he exemplified the local masculine values of aggression and toughness. Other boys later remembered him as the first to be picked for any team game. In his last year at school he become the captain of the rugby team (in the English game that had been imported into south Wales and rapidly assumed national importance). Davies enjoyed watching Wales play rugby all his life. As a boy he was also a good fighter, and he reports that his uncles on his mother's Welsh side of the family were delighted when he appeared still bearing the signs of his last fight. Davies proudly wrote how they predicted a career for him as a professional fighter, and perhaps they saw a way for the boy to win money and fame through the south-east Wales enthusiasm for prize fighting. It would have been a brutal route to success, but it is a reminder of the intensely masculine, working-class culture in which Davies was brought up. His ability as a fighter formed an important part of his sense of his masculinity.

Davies left school in 1885, aged fourteen, and began working for an ironmonger. The following May his grandfather died aged seventy-six. On 25 November 1886, at his grandmother's persuasion, he signed the indentures for a five-year apprenticeship to Jeremiah Williams, picture-frame carver and gilder, which included among its conditions a prohibition on frequenting taverns and playhouses. Respectability beckoned, along with financial security, but Davies was unenthusiastic. His energies were running towards educational self-improvement. Despite his revolt against his grandparents' morality, a year after he had left school he became an active member, along with his friend Dave Rees, of the Mutual Improvement Class at his grandmother's Baptist Church. Davies's poem entitled 'A Stormscape' was recited at the class, and it was later published in the *Monmouthshire Merlin* and *South Wales Advertiser* on 27 February 1887. He managed to combine self-improvement with rebellion when he delivered a paper 'In Defence of the Stage' to the class, drawing on his experience of visits to

Newport theatres such as the Lyceum and Empire made in defiance of his grandmother's views and the terms of his indentures. In the *Autobiography* Davies presents himself as a feckless apprentice, unwilling 'to apply myself sufficiently to that business so as to become a good workman'. His attention was focused instead, he writes, on his 'passion for reading'. His life seems to have been split between the boring work of his trade and the reading of English literature which he found so compelling.

In 1888, when he was seventeen, Davies met a young woman from a village near Newport who encouraged him in his intellectual pursuits. Little else is known about their relationship, but Davies recalled it in remarkable terms in the second chapter of the *Autobiography*, when he wrote that 'Her encouragement at that early time has been the star on which these eyes have seldom closed, by which I have successfully navigated the deeps of misery' (*AST* 30). The woman had died while still young, a year or so after they met. Davies remembers her in romantic terms, transformed into a far distant and inaccessible star which has since enabled him to plot his course in the hazardous journey of his life. Davies's words perhaps recall Sir Philip Sidney's sonnet sequence, *Astrophil and Stella* (1591), in which the loved woman is Stella (star) who, like most objects of erotic desire in Elizabethan sonnet sequences, arouses passionate desire but refuses sexual fulfilment, and whom the lover regards as far superior to himself, yet who offers only the remote possibility of total emotional and sexual bliss. The young woman's death revisited on Davies the association of love and loss that he had already experienced in the childhood death of his father and loss of his mother, and may have given him further cause to fear loving another person, especially a woman who could arouse his sexual passion. His romanticising of this young woman preserves her in memory as asexual and absent but an immensely powerful female influence. Loving a woman is only imaginable by representing her as an inaccessible, romantic ideal. Davies's relations with other women, frequently with prostitutes, involved simply the exchange of sexual pleasure, a relationship much simpler than the romance one. But the romantic idealising of women that Davies locates in his life story first appears here, and it persists through his life and his writing until the time when these two aspects of his erotic imagination are brought together in his extraordinary marriage.

In 1891, at the age of twenty, Davies completed his apprenticeship in frame-making. Although he disliked the work, it gave him an introduction to visual art that was to develop into real interest later in his life. Sybil Hollingdrake's research has uncovered Davies's efforts to establish an independent life for himself following his apprenticeship. He asked his grandmother for money to go to the United States, but when this request was refused he set out for London with only one sovereign. He managed to survive for four weeks, but had a miserable time of what he called in *Beggars* 'the worst side of life' in London doss-houses, and in the end had to write home asking for money. On his return to Wales he accepted a job with his master, the frame-maker. The desire to leave home persisted, and four months later, when he reached the age of twenty-one, he again asked his grandmother to support his emigration to the USA and was again refused. However, he did leave home in late 1892, crossing the Severn to Bristol and finding work there in his trade of picture-framing. During the next six months in Bristol he lived a life of alcoholic and sexual excess in the pubs and brothels of the slum area of the city known as the Pity. During these months he abandoned his intellectual pursuits, and behaved in ways that risked wrecking 'the brains and health of any man beyond recovery'. When in March 1893 his grandmother died, he was forced to return to Newport, 'a recall which Davies later described as having saved his life' (*ST* 14). Davies may again have been exaggerating in order to highlight the drama of his life, and of course it is common for young people of twenty-one to behave excessively in defiance of their parents' moral values. But in Davies's behaviour there seems to be something more than merely self-indulgence overturning nonconformist morality. During these months in Bristol what becomes apparent for the first time is his capacity for self-destruction. He probably was not exaggerating when, in opposition to the benign influence of the memory of the dead young woman as a 'star', he identified drink as 'my first officer, who many a day and many a night endeavoured to founder me'. Davies was a man driven by powerful, at times dangerous, feelings both towards others and himself. In a poem of 1918, originally entitled 'To the Woman who will read this Poem to her Husband', he presents himself somewhat ironically as a man unsuited to become a husband owing to his sensuality, immorality and devilish impulses:

> Thank heaven thou didst not marry me,
>   A poet full of the blackest evil;
> For how to manage my damned soul
>   Will puzzle many a flaming devil. (*PP*)

Amusing as it is, the poem very likely expresses some truth about how Davies saw himself and how he actually was.

Lydia Davies had invested money in property, and her will specified that the executor should not sell or mortgage it but rather divide the rents among the three children. As Hollingdrake observes, the will 'had been carefully designed to protect [the children] from their own weaknesses' (*ST* 15). William Henry Davies thus acquired an unearned income of ten shillings a week, and in a very small way become a *rentier*, though with hardly enough to live on comfortably. Although I have been referring to Davies's upbringing as 'working-class', his grandfather's occupation of inn-keeping and his grandmother's owning property put them into the thin social stratum of the Victorian lower middle class, consisting of shop-keepers, small employers, clerks, and innkeepers, who often lived among the predominant working class to whose ranks economic insecurity might easily return them. Davies's class position thus became borderline. When he was living in the USA as a tramp and beggar he must have been one of the few with a private income. Mary Ann Hill, the Davies children's estranged mother, offered them shelter after their grandmother's death. During the intervening eighteen years she had had four children by her second husband who had died while her second family was still young. A third marriage too had ended in widowhood. In the course of this hard life she had survived periods of poverty by plying her father's trade of cobbler and shoemaker. She was remembered as 'a calm, strong-willed woman who could neither be daunted nor surprised' (*ST* 15). In 1893 she took on responsibility for her three first children, thinking especially of the simple-minded Francis whom she continued to look after. The third child Matilda also joined her mother and her half-siblings. Eventually she was to abandon her husband and five children and move to Canada, and part of this life story found its way into Davies's novel, *A Weak Woman*. William Henry seems to have gladly renewed close contact with his mother and her family. He became a close and long-lasting friend of his half-sister Alice who has been described as having, like her mother and Davies himself, 'unusual alien features', being short and broad-shouldered with a large head, sensuous lips and deep-set eyes. Welsh family values – closeness, mutual responsibility, solidarity in the face of adversity – were brought into play by Davies's mother. But Davies found the closeness of family life stifling, its responsibility endless. Three months after his grandmother's death he had negotiated an advance of fifteen pounds from her executor and set sail for freedom and independence from Liverpool in June 1893.

Why did Davies emigrate to the USA in 1893? It was certainly not for economic survival or self-advancement, for south Wales was still booming in the 1890s, and in that decade the population of Wales actually increased. There had been decades when Welsh people did emigrate to the USA in the 1790s, 1860s, and in the crisis of the rural economy of the 1880s, but the 1890s saw little emigration. The economic success of industrial south Wales in the period up to 1921 made the Welsh 'the least emigration-prone of all the peoples of the British Isles'. In that period there were 77 per 10,000 Irish immigrants to north America, 20 Scots, 12 English but only 3 Welsh. As Gwyn Williams wrote, 'the Welsh did not need to emigrate' (*WWW* 179-80). But W.H. Davies did, though not for economic reasons. His reasons were personal. He was a man of twenty-two years, without plans for marriage and establishing a home of his own, and no enthusiasm for a lifetime of work at his trade. 'Home', the bulwark of working-class life, had not offered him security: his first home had been shattered by his father's death and his mother's remarriage: and the abnormal home provided by his grandparents had disappeared with their deaths. His mother's home could provide only temporary refuge. Lacking a secure home led him to look elsewhere for a place to live, and to seek security and a sense of self-identity in other kinds of human relationships. When he emigrated he began decades of moving from place to place. The idea of home, however, remained strong in his writing. In 'Old Times' in the first published volume, *The Soul's Destroyer* (1905), he writes how the breaking up of old homes 'Is ache and breaking to my heart –/New homes keep chilly hearths for me'. The word 'home' still had romance for him.

Two: Tramp, Cripple and Literary Ambition 1893-1905

From June 1893, when he set sail for the United States, till June 1899, when he returned for the last time to Britain, Davies travelled from place to place in America, sometimes working for brief periods, sometimes begging; and also crossed the Atlantic several times working as a sailor on cattle ships. Despite the best efforts of his biographer Richard Stonesifer (himself North American) to track Davies's movements during these years, it is impossible to follow his life in detail or, more importantly, to learn much about what it meant for him as he was experiencing it. Sybil Hollingdrake has calculated that only five of Davies's poems deal directly with north America: 'The White Cascade', 'The Rock', 'Music', 'Song of Life', and 'Wonderful Places'; and Stonesifer comments that the impression we get of this six-year period in Davies's life is 'a highly selective one, for he omitted much' (*WHDB* 26). Certainly, it is unwise to turn to Davies's accounts of these years for a reliable chronology or an accurate record of his life: *The Autobiography of a Super-Tramp* (1908), *Beggars* (1909), *The True Traveller* (1912), *The Adventures of Johnny Walker, Tramp* (1926, but mostly drawn from the 1909 and 1912 books). Amazingly, in the first draft of the *Autobiography* Davies made no mention of his years in the States, and it was only after his bowdlerisation of this draft made it too short that he wrote about these years. And yet Davies's biographer has few other sources to work from, so Davies's accounts, reshaped and varnished as they certainly are, still provide the main source for his life during these years.

Davies travelled to the United States with the tools of his picture-framing trade but he never worked as a picture-framer. The 1890s in the United States were depression years. Hockey records how

Davies abandoned his tools in lieu of rent at a lodging house soon after he reached New York, and never again worked at his trade. Davies was always averse to the constraints and oppressions of a regular job, though he did try, but failed, to find a job when he landed. What he wanted was 'merely ... to be free' (*WHDB* 28), though that did not solve the problem of how to live. According to his biographer, 'he was not a born adventurer either', and he had no intention, when he left Wales, of dropping out of society and living as a tramp and beggar; it was 'as a result of circumstances and necessity' that he fell into that way of life. Certainly, this was not an easy path to follow.

He was in New York only a short time, then went to Connecticut to see friends of friends. At this crucial juncture we have to depend on Davies's own account of sitting on a park bench and asking a man sitting near him how much it would cost to take the train to Chicago. The stranger asked if he was planning to 'beat' his way there, and noticing Davies's incomprehension, explained that that meant jumping on freight trains for a free ride. The man, named Brum, then offered to travel with Davies himself, and Davies readily agreed. Over the next few months Brum inducted him into his sub-culture of professional begging, and taught him how to survive and thrive as a beggar in the USA.

What is significant in the way Davies tells this story is the protagonist's passivity. With no burning ambition to do anything in particular (for example, go west, become rich, marry and have children, become a writer) Davies represents himself as responding positively to the first chance suggestion for action that's put to him. This allows him not to have to take responsibility for his subsequent actions, and puts him on the margins of the subculture he has fallen into. This is a good vantage point for a future writer, but it may well have been constructed by the protagonist-turned-writer after the event. According to his own account, Davies spent the summer of 1893 along the Long Island Sound with Brum as his companion. In New Haven, he was jailed for thirty days as a vagrant. After brief spells of work wood-cutting and working in hop fields, he travelled at Brum's suggestion to Michigan to spend the winter in local jails where a scam gave beggars shelter, and the local marshal, judge and sheriff all received payment for every man jailed from the local taxes of unsuspecting citizens. When he emerged from the winter of 1893-4 in various jails, Davies turned in the summer of 1894 to fruit picking on a farm near St Joseph, Michigan owned by a German couple who offered to adopt him at the end of the season. Having saved a hundred dollars during this time, he wanted to return to Britain, and so travelled to Chicago, but when he arrived there he and his companion known as Australian Red blew the money in a week of wild debauch. And so they decided to beat their way to Baltimore where they signed on as labourers on a cattle ship sailing to Liverpool. In describing these events Davies is happy to let himself appear as indecisive and easily swayed by the impulse to physical pleasure. He seems too to have little commitment to larger plans, for he planned to return to Britain and stay, but in a few days he changed his mind and returned to Baltimore. Once again, in October 1894, he signed up on a cattle ship, this time to Glasgow; and later again he sailed from Baltimore to London, staying in Southwark and enjoying the culture available for free in London parks, museums, and art galleries. In his first eighteen months in America Davies seems to have created the freedom he sought by piecing together a life from widely different fragments: as a beggar, brief spells of outdoor manual work, the hard life on cattle ships, and spells of reading and encountering high culture. He was free from the depressing routines of a regular job but his life among tramps and hobos was hard, dangerous, and at times violent.

Davies spent Christmas 1894 in Baltimore, revelling in the quantities of rich food begged from generous householders by him and other tramps for their Christmas feast. The story suggests a generosity of spirit among Americans of that time towards some of the country's poor and down-and-outs. Davies's travels over the next three years cannot be traced exactly, though we know that he moved to Chicago, probably in 1895 to work on the digging of a canal. In his account of this period in his autobiography, he brings out the brutality of the situation in the labour camp among the men working there and of gangs of other men who attacked them. Some men died from the dangerous work, but many others were killed by the marauding gangs. Davies would work for a short time saving enough money for a blow-out in a big city; and after working on the canal he went to Chicago and spent the fifty dollars he had saved on drink. This probably happened in early 1895, but from then until mid-1898 it is not possible to trace Davies's travels in the United States in exact detail. Even Davies's assiduous biographer, Richard Stonesifer, has been able to identify only certain periods of travel during these three years, and in order to do this he has had to draw his information from Davies's unreliable autobiographies. From Davies's patchy and sometimes overlapping accounts it becomes apparent that he must have travelled south to St Louis, then sailed further south with a group of other white tramps on a boat on the Mississippi. He contracted a serious bout of malaria, and at one stage, near-delirious with fever, he collapsed not far from the rail tracks and did not have the strength to move for several days. Eventually, he did manage to reach a railway station and board a train to Memphis where he reached a charity hospital and was taken in and nursed back to health. After this it seems he travelled down to New Orleans. At other times during these years he 'wandered on, across Arkansas, Mississippi, Louisiana, Texas, crossing and recross-ing these states' (*WHDB* 35). It is worth noticing the extent of Davies's travels across the States because of how little impression it seems to have left on his writing or on his imagination. Perhaps because of his position outside respectable American society, and the consequent rough and dangerous life he led, or because he had no contact with the positive values of American society, or because he came to see his time in the States as wasted, he did not draw on his American experience in his writing except as a string of mostly alien and damaging encounters with the people and the land. Certainly, by 1898 he was coming to feel the futility of his life in the States.

During the summer of 1898 he worked in Illinois as a fruit picker, then went to Chicago with the money he had earned to enjoy himself, as he usually did, with drink and women and going to theatres. After three weeks of this he claims, one Sunday, to have experienced a moment of self-recrimination for wasted time and an idea of how his life might have been. The narrative in the *Autobiography* reads like an episode from a Victorian melodrama or a temperance pamphlet, and it probably presents as a dramatic turning-point a change in Davies that may actually have been more gradual:

> One Sunday, I had bought a weekly paper, wherein I read an appreciation of the poet Burns, with numerous quotations from his work. My thoughts wandered back to the past, the ambition of my early days, and the encouraging work of my elders. 'Ah,' I said, with a sigh, 'if during these five years I had had the daily companionship of good books, instead of all this restless wandering to and fro in a strange land, my mind, at the present hour, might be capable of some little achievement of its own.' (*AST* 120-21)

Robert Burns is an appropriate poet for Davies to have identified with since he too came from a lower-class family, was largely self-educated, and he enjoyed drinking and sex; and Burns' national reputation as a poet was achieved despite being a Scot far from the centres of cultural dominance in Edinburgh and London. Burns' career traced a path from social obscurity that Davies could identify with, to national poetic fame that he could project as a career for himself. In his story of reading about Burns we see the first stirrings in Davies of an active response to his own life, or at least the preliminary dissatisfaction with his present circumstances. Many of the stories he tells about his adventures in America depict himself as at times the almost comically passive object of other peoples' actions. Having apparently decided to leave the United States and start his life afresh in Britain, he travelled to Baltimore, his home port, to work his way to Britain on a cattle boat, but when he arrived there he fell into a familiar pattern, meeting Australian Red and spending all his money, earned over the summer, on a drinking binge. No sudden transformation then, but it seems that Davies had resolved to return to Newport and change the direction of his life. The thirty shillings he earned as a sailor bought him new clothes in Liverpool, and he returned to Newport in 1898.

His two months in Newport were not happy. He showed up at his mother's house and was taken in. He began to live off the £150 that he had accumulated from his grandmother's legacy. But he was unhappy and began drinking heavily. The old friends that he met had settled into jobs that were a far cry from his life as a tramp: Dave Rees had become a foreman in a foundry. Davies took work on a ship sailing to Bordeaux. But he had no clear idea of what to do next. The idea of starting a bookshop in London occurred to him, and he went to London to put this plan into action, and spent more of his money during a week of walking the streets and going to theatres. At last he found a way out of the impasse when he read in the newspaper of the Klondike gold rush in Alaska. He changed thirty pounds of his rapidly dwindling wealth into Canadian dollars, lodged them in a money belt round his waist, and travelled to Canada to beat his way to Alaska. When he sailed to Canada is uncertain (and Davies's biographer calls the *Autobiography* completely unreliable about this point in his life) but we know on 20 March 1899 Davies and another tramp were in the Canadian Pacific station at Renfrew, Ontario waiting to steal a ride on a train going to Winnipeg. This was the night when the accident occurred that led to the amputation of Davies's leg, the momentous event which was to be the turning-point of his life. He and the other tramp, called Three-fingered Jack, had found that they had hitched a ride on a train that deposited them no further west than Renfrew, and so had to ride on another train to get them on their way to the Klondike. The obliging chief of police of Renfrew had given them shelter in the cells on the night of 19 March, and the next day they were to jump aboard the express to Winnipeg. Davies let Three-Fingered Jack jump first because of his disabled hand, and he jumped next, but because the train was travelling so fast by this time he missed his footing and was dragged under the wheels for some distance before he let go. When he came to and examined himself he found that his right foot was severed. A report in the local newspaper, the *Renfrew Mercury* of 24 March 1899, gives an account of Davies's reaction to this horrific accident with heroic indifference:

> ... he lay in the snow for some time, but finally his cries attracted Mr. Jas. Galvin, who went to investigate, and soon had the victim of the accident in the station. Here he displayed wonderful nerve, and informed the authorities that he had money on his person. When the Chief appeared, the sufferer saluted him with, 'Well, Chief, I've been done up! It's my own fault! I had the money to pay my way, but tried to save it.' He had $143 dollars sewed about his clothes. This he handed to the Chief, as well as his razor and knife, saying as to the latter that one never knew what might

happen ... Drs. Connolly and Murphy were summoned and ban-
daged the foot at the station, preparatory to having the man
removed to the hospital. While the bandaging was in progress,
Davies took out his pipe and had a smoke. At the hospital, the
Doctors amputated the left [*sic*] foot at the ankle ... throughout
Davies exhibited such fortitude that Dr. Connolly remarked that
it was easy to understand how Britishers won victories, if they
were made of such stuff as he was. (*WHDB* 40)

Davies's courage and self-possession are impressive, and the fact
that this report comes not from his autobiography but from the local
newspaper gives it all the more credibility. His heroism is certainly
real and independently attested, and it manifests itself in Davies's
bravura performance. This accident is the crucial event that after
several years of struggle was to turn Davies into a writer; but it is
also the moment when we see in his life story for the first time and
in a highly dramatic way Davies's powers of artful self-fashioning.
What the newspaper reports is Davies's shrewd, practical responses,
telling his rescuers that he has money to pay for medical care,
accounting to the Chief for the knife he carries, and, most strikingly,
displaying his courage as a show of indifference to the catastrophe
that had befallen him. When the doctor says that his *sang froid* was
an example of the British pluck that has won victories, Davies is personally validated not as an insignificant, deracinated tramp but as a
social type, the brave Britisher. It is remarkable that this accident
seems instantly to release in Davies his powers of self-realisation. It
would be years before that process of forging a social identity would
be complete, but this is the moment when it begins.

His identity was always complex. There were occasions when,
reaching a city with a library, he would spend time there reading
books. This sense of Davies being somewhat uneasy in the subculture
of tramps and beggars can be observed, according to Hollingdrake,
in the pages of the *Autobiography* and *Beggars*. She believes that
Davies wanted to project an image of himself as a tramp in the States
as a devil-may-care adventurer, and so he tells his stories with 'a tren-
chant simplicity' meant to give this impression. But he admits that
other beggars sometimes derided him as a '"shovel-stiff, cattle-stiff,
or barrel-house stiff" (in other words a navvy, cattle-boat worker, or
man who touted for free drinks in taverns)'. Davies's accounts of his

life as a vagrant suggest that he was 'never completely absorbed into the vagrant's way of life' (*ST* 17), but that to survive and thrive in it he had to project a certain identity that only showed part of what he might be. The tramps' derisive names for Davies when he occasionally worked show the difficulty of fighting for a place in the tramp world. Before the moment arrived when he found himself grievously wounded in the railroad accident, Davies had been practising the arts of survival through constructing a convincing self.

Chapter 10, 'The Cattleman's Office', is one of the best chapters of the *Autobiography*, in which Davies temporarily turns away from himself as the book's central concern, and focuses on the trans-Atlantic trade in the transport of live cattle, and particularly the behaviour of the animals themselves. His compassionate reactions to the cattle ships are at odds with the other cattlemen's callousness, and by the end of this chapter he is representing himself as wanting to break free of the vagrant's life and turn to books. He describes the cattle being driven up the gangway on to the ship and being 'unmercifully prodded with long poles, sharpened at the end, and used by the shore cattlemen'. He recognises the animals' sufferings and the men's cruelty, and his own repulsion at the scene:

> The terror-stricken animals were so new to the conditions, that they had no notion of what was expected of them, and almost overleaped one another in their anxiety to get away. What with the shout of savage triumph, and the curse of disappointment, and the slipping and falling of the over-goaded steers, I was strongly tempted to escape the scene. (*AST* 76)

The effectiveness of this chapter lies not only in Davies's strong personal reactions to what goes on in the cattle ship, but in his sense of the exploitation of men as well as cattle; both are at the mercy of larger forces. The men have to wait for days or weeks in Baltimore for work, and the work is hard and dangerous, dealing with cattle breaking loose from their tethers or collapsed owing to being allowed to rest too long on their knees. Davies tells how, out of kindness for a big, black steer, he let it rest too long during his shift but then found it could not move. He recounts how its tail is twisted, it is prodded with a pitchfork 'which must have gone an inch into the body', and is only raised to its feet by the agonising pain of 'a large chew of tobacco' being placed deliberately 'on one of the animal's eyes'. He writes that his heart sickened and that he 'would have to be less gentle with these poor creatures to save them the worst of cruelty'. He recognises that he is compelled to act cruelly. And he also sees that the cattlemen become 'great thieves' of food because the company allowed

> their stewards such miserly small amounts for provisions, that the common sailors and firemen did not get sufficient food to eat, bad as its quality was.

Davies's attitude to his fellow cattlemen is a complex mixture of compassion and clear-eyed judgement. He describes them as 'the scum of America, a wild, lawless class of people', but he sees clearly how they will be 'unscrupulously' imposed on by 'the scum of Europe' by having their generosity exploited. America is prosperous compared to the 'extreme poverty' of Liverpool, and begging there an easy enterprise:

> These wild, but kind-hearted men ... give and give of their few shillings, until they themselves are reduced to the utmost want.

Davies observes the cultural differences like a social anthropologist, but not an objective one, for he is involved in the scene he represents. His own generosity towards the men left with no money is activated – 'In such cases, who could help but attend to them at once, before attempting to enjoy his own meal?' – but the result is that he spends all his thirty shillings of wages from the voyage. He writes that he had eschewed drink and gone instead to a library where he indulged his 'old passion for reading', but helping his fellows left him with nothing to buy books for himself. In this unusually coherent chapter the conflicting forces in Davies's life at this time are evident. He works in a harsh world alongside men whose crudity or simplicity he can recognise, and at the same time he wants to read. Yet his own sympathy and involvement with these men makes him behave in ways that frustrate his desire for something better. At this stage of his life all he can express is his frustrated hope to 'make better arrangements for the future'. But he has no notion of how to make those better arrangements. The amputation of Davies's right foot caused him great suffering despite the bravado with which he initially reacted to the trauma. In the *Autobiography* he writes that the 'outward fortitude' he displayed 'was far from the true state of my feelings'; and it was the sudden transformation from being a strong, athletic man to his 'present helplessness' that caused him 'many a bitter moment' (*AST* 143). The directness and understatement of Davies's writing about his accident strikes the reader as an authentic account of his predicament. He barely mentions the physical pain he must have endured, which was so great that in his struggles he opened the wound on his leg and made a second amputation on his right leg necessary, this time above the knee. We have two sources of information about Davies's accident: his own *Autobiography*, and two articles and a letter of Davies's in the *Renfrew Mercury* in March and May 1899, and all of these documents are informative. Bernard Shaw reacted to Davies's writing in these passages, in the Preface he wrote for the *Autobiography*, drawing attention to 'the extraordinary quietness of his narrative' which might seem like 'monstrous callousness', the reaction to the loss of a limb seeming no more marked than how 'a lobster loses a claw or a lizard his tail'. But, as Stonesifer says, Davies was 'very shrewd in calculating his effects, [and] worked very deliberately for this extraordinary quietness in narration' (*WHDB* 42). Davies's account of his accident and recovery has strands of humour and pathos running through it. When he is first taken to the hospital and is sinking into chloroformed unconsciousness, he lets out, he writes, a stream of foul language which he is later assured is common at such moments, but which he wonders if the matron had heard 'and if she had confided in her daughter'. This odd sexual daydream fantasises a relation between the sixteen-year old girl, described as 'womanly and considerate', and the twenty-seven year old beggar on the basis of filthy language, and it seems both comic and serious: comic in the disparity between foul-mouthed tramp and respectable matron and daughter, and serious in imagining desire being transmitted by such unlikely means. There are strong feelings ambiguously stirred by Davies's writing here, but when he mentions his departure from the matron a few paragraphs later the feelings are conventionally expressed, though equally powerful: the matron 'Put her two hands on my shoulders and kissed me, her eyes being full of tears'. Davies responds with equal intensity: 'I felt my voice gone, and my throat in the clutches of something new to my experience'. This is one of the few moments in the *Autobiography* when strong feeling is directly represented, and it is part of the rapid sketch artfully composed of fragments of action and reaction. The paragraph about the matron's and Davies's emotions on parting ends with the heartfelt understatement that the people of the town of Renfrew were 'true friends'.

The lightness with which Davies treated his accident, both in his life and his writing, concealed his realisation that the event was momentous. The amputation left him crippled and deprived of his much-prized physical prowess; he had come close to dying; and the prospect of making his fortune in the Klondyke had disappeared. He published a letter of thanks to the people of Renfrew in the local newspaper in his bravado style. It contained, however, a serio-comic allusion to God's predestination that suggests Davies's sombre sense of the accident's significance:

> If I believe in predestination, I must certainly thank the Creator of all things, for picking out such a good spot in the universe for the accomplishment of His work (*WHDB* 42).

This is a joke (though Davies's grandmother would have approved the theological sentiment) which would prove to be true. Davies seized on his accident and turned his personal disaster into the opportunity for recreating himself. The story of his life that the *Autobiography* tells seems to prove that the accident was indeed part of a larger story that would lead on through disaster to far greater success. Davies left Canada in May 1899 and by the next month had returned to Newport to live with his mother. By the time he was in Wales he was writing poetry, and went so far as to submit some to publishers, though without success. He had bought an artificial leg from a London supplier for the considerable sum of £12. 10. 0. Some time between being in hospital in Canada and reaching Newport again he had struck upon the extraordinary and unlikely idea of becoming a poet. In his personal mythology it was reading about

Robert Burns that fired this ambition, and indeed Davies later changed the story of having read the article on Burns in Chicago to having read it in hospital in Renfrew so that his transformation might seem all the more sudden, rather like a story of religious conversion. In any case Davies decided to live in London in order to realise his ambition. His grandmother's legacy of ten shillings a week would be sufficient to sustain a poor life in a working man's lodging house, while the essential activity of writing went on. In August 1899 Davies went to live in a doss house in Blackfriars Road but it was badly run and the lodgers were drunken. He then moved to Rowton House in Newington Butts where there was more order, along with a quiet library with two bookcases containing fiction, poetry, history, essays, and biography. Lodgings there cost sixpence a night leaving only six shillings and sixpence a week for everything else. Davies claims in his autobiography, and it seems reasonable to believe him, that he had to live extremely frugally and to renounce most of his pleasures, except tobacco, in order to afford to stay in Rowton House. He renounced drink, and going to theatres, and even had to renounce what he slyly calls 'other indoor entertainments', presumably sexual, while he committed himself to writing. He lived in Rowton House for two years.

Davies's notion of what kind of writing would succeed in the late 1890s was bizarre. Had he been writing in the 1590s he might have had some success with 'a tragedy, written in blank verse' called *The Robber* (now lost) which was, he claims, full of action. This was written in two months and rejected by a publisher in three days. In the *Autobiography*, the only source for our knowledge of how Davies spent these years, he takes great delight in depicting himself as a literary innocent: 'My conceit, at this time,' he writes, 'was foolish in the extreme, and yet I was near my thirtieth year' (*AST* 152). He wrote in archaic genres that he had encountered in his reading. A medieval beast fable had the world's fauna gathering to condemn man for his cruelty to them, and their midnight journey 'to the nearest town, and the vengeance they then took on the sleeping inhabitants'. A sequence of a hundred Elizabethan sonnets followed, their demanding form providing useful technical practice; then 'another tragedy, a comedy, a volume of humorous essays, and hundreds, I believe, of short poems' (*AST* 153). What Davies wrote in his first year in London shows how remote he was from the contemporary literary scene, and how little sense he had of the literary market. Over a brief period of time he was recapitulating in his writing a series of out-dated or defunct literary forms – humorous essays probably followed his reading Charles Lamb – but at the same time he was practising his craft, so that by some time in 1900 he had assembled enough short poems to form a recognisable volume of saleable poetry. A publisher to whom this collection was sent offered to publish it provided that Davies covered the costs of twenty-five pounds but Davies did not have so much money. He wrote to six people known to support good causes asking for their assistance, but with no success. He then conceived a plan that he hoped would earn him enough to take up the publisher's offer. He decided to print three or four of his short poems on a single sheet and sell them round the doors, hoping to make enough profit to allow him to have his volume published. Thirty five shillings was the cost of this print-ing job, a sum he managed to raise by extreme self-deprivation. But his attempts to sell these sheets 'in the suburbs of London' was met with incomprehension or refusal: 'All these people did was to stare, none of them seeming to understand, and no one seemed inclined to ask questions'. (*AST* 154). His response to this humiliating failure was, he tells us, an outburst of destructive rage: returning to Rowton House he began 'with the fury of a madman, to burn the copies, and did not rest until they were all destroyed, taking care not to save one copy that would at any time in the future remind me of my folly' (*AST* 155). The rage that erupts here is a significant part of Davies's personality, and it reappears several times in the course of his life story. He calls his rage intense and beyond the bounds of reason, breaking out when the folly and unreality of his plans to peddle his poems are revealed to him. His burning anger is closely connected to his burning ambition, for the ambition, certainly at this moment of his life, is driven by a fantasy of literary success that would seem to be as futile and unrealistic as selling poems round the doors. The 'fury of a madman' is a phrase as appropriate to describe the way he was writing during this year as to describe the burning of the unsold sheets. Davies was a man of very powerful emotions who felt that his place in the world was far from assured, and when his insecurity was activated then his passions were liable to erupt.

This failure was followed by further hardships. Davies carried on writing and reading during 1900, but some time in 1901 he decided that out of his income of ten shillings a week he would give part of it to 'one who would be thankful of a couple of shillings a week'. What he off-handedly called in his autobiography 'a little sacrifice' in fact deprived him of a quarter of his income and required him to move from the relative comfort of Rowton House, with its library for reading and writing, to the squalor of a Salvation Army hostel called The Ark, in Southwark Street. It is not known who the recipient of Davies's charity was, though Stonesifer thought it might have been his mother or brother Frank, and Hollingdrake speculated along romantic lines that it might have been an old girlfriend in Wales recently widowed. In any case the result was further material deprivation and more difficult conditions in which to write. It was indeed what Hollingdrake calls 'an act of awesome generosity' (*ST* 20) and at the same time it was an intensification of his self-imposed suffering. As Davies's literary ambitions strengthened (ambitions that any reasonable person at the time would surely have declared hopeless) so the material conditions that might help realise those ambitions became sharply less favourable. Davies's life at this time was surely a desperate gamble, its fate poised between artistic success and wordly recognition, and deeper humiliation and social extinction among the outcasts of the world. The fact that Davies was eventually successful seems to vindicate his gamble, but at the time he was gambling with his very existence.

With his weekly income reduced to six shillings a week, Davies moved to The Ark in 1901, where he paid two shillings a week rent, and lived there for two years, a period punctuated by a spell on the road in the Midlands of England in late 1902. Davies loathed the Salvation Army religiosity of The Ark, along with the petty corruption of some of the officials there. Living conditions were much worse than at Rowton House: inmates were compelled to leave the building from 10.00 a.m. to 1.00 p.m. every day, and the beds were placed so close together in the dormitory that no privacy was possible. An unusual note of indignation appears in Davies's account of this period in the *Autobiography*; usually, he is content to describe scenes without overt comment, but in his chapter on The Ark he directly condemns the institution and the people who ran it. 'The officers in charge,' he writes, 'were hypocrites', and he deftly represents the Lieutenant's sneaking compliance with the Captain. He captures the Captain's empty sermonising by a skilfully told story of disappearing Horace, who first prompted a bravura funeral sermon from the Captain –

> The Captain wept copiously, being overcome by his feelings, and the Lieutenant approved and encouraged him by an unusual number of sighs and broken sobs (*AST* 158)

and then, when Horace unexpectedly reappeared, he was received by the Captain and his toadying Lieutenant with irritation and thereafter disregard. Davies's writing here has a comic flair that suggests he learned a lot from Dickens, including his condemnation of cruel institutions. The men were ejected daily from the building, did not have the facilities to keep themselves clean, and were given no charity by the Army. 'Whatever good the Salvation Army did for the homeless and penniless in their shelters', Davies writes,

> they certainly did not cater well for these poor, but independent, fellows whose wages ranged from a shilling to eighteen pence a day – being paper-men, sandwichmen, toy-sellers etc. (*AST* 160).

Davies, of course, did none of those things but continued to scrape by on the residue of his income and to write. With no library like that at Rowton House he was forced to try to work either in local libraries, where he was treated with suspicion by the librarians, or in the crowded, raucous kitchen of the hostel. In *Beggars*, his second book of autobiographical recollections of his years on the road, he recalls how he tried to write in The Ark's kitchen, but it was 'with the utmost difficulty that I could concentrate my thoughts'. He therefore resorted to subterfuge, sitting in a corner and pretending to be asleep: 'By these means I often managed to compose a poem, which I would commit to paper before I went to bed' (*B* 185). By this process of mental composition, he claims, he wrote most of the poems in *The Soul's Destroyer*.

Deeper humiliation followed when his artificial leg began to disintegrate and he was forced to seek funds for a replacement from the Surgical Aid Society. Again, the account Davies gives in his autobiography is uncharacteristically condemnatory, which suggests that the Society's suspicious questioning of him and his circumstances had bitten deep. He had to pay sixpence for a subscription book that contained the names of possible benefactors. Davies had to obtain letters promising subscriptions from fifteen of these people, and so himself had to spend money and effort in sending begging letters. It was summer and many potential subscribers were on holiday; and the Boer War was also producing injured ex-servicemen needing help. But eventually Davies's letters produced the fifteen subscribers needed, and Davies acquired a new peg leg, sturdier than the metal and leather contraption he had first been fitted with. The goal of publication could only be reached by gathering the money needed to pay for publication, and to do that Davies needed to save money from his tiny income. He decided to live as a tramp for a few months, and so save his income towards the thirty pounds needed for publishing his book. Although the chronology of Davies's life in this period is still uncertain, it seems likely that it was in September 1902 that he set off, having registered as a hawker with the police, to beg outside London. It was too late in the year to think of a six-month period of saving money by sleeping rough; and it was damp weather that soon ruined the stock of pins and shoe laces he was hawking. He survived as a beggar until Christmas but the experience was miserable, for as Stonesifer observes, the 'more he had to beg, the less he liked begging' (*WHDB* 51). Davies's success in begging in the States had depended a good deal on the generosity people there showed to beggars but also to Davies's deployment of his young man's charm, especially towards housewives. Now that charm had disappeared to be replaced by the pitiful spectacle of being a cripple, but Davies refused to 'stand pad' and use his disability as a way of extracting money from passers-by. But he also found himself unable to deploy the necessary verbal dexterity, or persistence, or even just the usual formulae, to make begging successful. His sense of himself made it difficult for him to play the role of beggar effectively, as he was well aware:

> The number of times people have called me back, after I have
> left their doors, and assisted me, has often proved to me how
> they had waited to have their first feelings of pity strengthened
> by some recital of poverty (*AST* 174).

He tramped through St Albans, Rugby, Coventry, Birmingham and
Warwick, staving in lodging houses as he went, and arrived at
Stratford-upon-Avon in November, to him 'this enchanted place' for
its associations with William Shakespeare. Like a castaway on a
desert island he carried with him the Bible and Shakespeare, along
with the manuscript of his own poems. When he reached a town
and had arranged a bed for the night in one of its lodging houses he
would make for the local public library to spend some time reading
and writing. The plan to accumulate funds as he went, however, had
failed, and as the weather worsened in December he made his way
to Newport for Christmas. He was in a poor physical condition after
four months of tramping; his wooden leg exhausted him, and his
'lack of food brought him close to collapse' (*WHDB* 55). It was his
proud boast that even during this period he escaped the degradation of the workhouse, so retaining the status, as Stonesifer says, of
a true traveller. But the daily necessity of getting the money to pay
for the night's lodging became increasingly desperate. He describes
how at this time he would beg people for money 'flourishing before
their eyes a whip of a dozen laces', intimidating them until he had
been given money, and then people could 'come and go without fear
of being molested'. Again it is the extremes of Davies's experience
that are so striking. It was what Davies calls his 'mad fit', the possibility of violence in him, that made people give him money. At the
same time he was suffering through these dreadful months; and
realised it. When he could not go on any further, so the
Autobiography records, he asked himself, 'why had I done this, and
to what end had I suffered?' (*AST* 182). Suffering, futility, the passions of a powerful personality, and the quest for an apparently
hopeless self-realisation are the motifs of these months. Returning to
Newport must have accentuated his failure, but he stayed there for
a month, regaining his strength, and then, having collected his
unspent income, tramped his way back to London in early 1903.

Back in London he could not face the squalor of The Ark again, and on the recommendation of friends moved to another lodging house, The Farmhouse in Marshalsea Road. There he seems to have found an orderly regime run by a manager and his wife, and, from the other lodgers, a degree of respect despite his seeming to be different from them. In *Autobiography* he writes that 'he did everything that these men dislike', such as wearing a white collar 'which they at once take to be a challenge that you are superior'; or using a toothbrush which 'few other men in the house, except they were fighting men, could have produced ... without being sneered at'; or being 'almost a teetotaller ... the worst charge of all'. This suggests that Davies had his own personal authority that these other rough men recognised. As he describes it, The Farmhouse seems to have offered him the kind of security that might have come from a family, but in his case did not. The place held two hundred men, but was kept, he writes, 'as quiet as a large mansion with its one small family and half a score of servants' (*AST* 190-1). If Davies's account is to be believed then his way of life had changed from his years as a tramp in north America. There he would work or beg, then blow the money on women and drink in the nearest big city. In The Farmhouse Davies seems to have resisted heavy drinking, and have begun to fashion a private, indeed secret, identity as a man guarding his privacy and exercising his powers as if he were a writer. The public recognition of that identity was what he was secretly struggling for.

In January 1904 Davies sent a manuscript of his poems to another publisher Clement K. Shorter, who rejected it. It was now over four years since he had first sent poems to a publisher in the hope of having them published, and his persistence – or was it obsession? – was remarkable. But Davies seems to have had no alternative future for himself except as a poet. He sent his manuscript 'to a literary man' asking for his judgement, but had the parcel returned. The manager of the hostel noticed Davies's parcel and 'the secret which [Davies] had guarded so jealously' was out. With this man's encouragement, however, Davies continued his efforts towards the magic moment of publication, now hoping that one of The Farmhouse's rich benefactors might come to his aid. He sent his manuscript to another publisher, this time Watts and Co., who replied with an offer to publish provided that he paid thirty pounds towards the cost. As he recounts events, Davies then trusted the manager to contact the hostel's benefactors and persuade them to contribute towards the thirty pounds necessary. Davies then expected the money to be easily raised by the manager, and 'with full trust in the man's goodness and influence, made myself comfortable, and settled down in a fool's paradise' (*AST* 198). Nothing happened for several weeks, and during that time Davies's hopelessness increased and he sank into a state of depression. In June 1904 he finally realised that he would have to act for himself, and turning once more to the resource that had made all of his ambitions realisable he travelled to Newport to negotiate with the trustee of his grandmother's estate a loan on his income. As he recounts them, the point of these ups and downs of hope and failure is to demonstrate that he had no reliable help except himself. The *Autobiography* shows Davies as being alternatively foolishly trusting in others and determinedly self-reliant, emphasising that the success he achieved came from himself alone. In Newport he failed to persuade the lawyer Jacob Waite, the trustee of his grandmother's estate, to lend him money, but managed to arrange that his income would be accumulated for six months, providing ten pounds, and then a loan of twenty pounds would be added, making the thirty pounds needed for publication. Foregoing his income meant that he would have to leave The Farmhouse and yet again survive for six months as a tramp and beggar. There is bitterness in the *Autobiography*'s words recalling this moment, for Davies leaves The Farmhouse and London resolved 'never to set foot in that house again until I could dispense with the services of others', and 'not knowing how much I would have to suffer' (*AST* 201). Davies's struggles to become a poet, a figure fashioned through loneliness and suffering, are a narrative of the romantic artist whose sufferings in some way authenticate the art he produces. Significantly, he does not represent himself as a working-class writer struggling in poverty and lack of education against publishers' demanding payment for publication. The story he tells depicts him as being impelled by a poetic vocation, and willing to undergo apparently endless suffering to realise it.

From June to December 1904 Davies spent his last, most difficult, period as a tramp and beggar. With the prospect of his life being transformed with his becoming a published author, he turned again to an old way of life that was experienced this time as something for which he was no longer suited and which had merely to be endured. Davies might have taken a job, but that was out of the question. It is a measure of his tunnel vision that he held the prize of authorship before his eyes and saw begging as the only way to reach it. Davies's biographers too have found themselves compelled to follow not only what he did during these months but how he interpreted it.

The picture that emerges in Chapter 28 of the *Autobiography* is of a man almost deranged by the pressures he was under. He had 'neither the courage to beg or sell'; he travelled alone with no-one to disturb his 'dreams'; and he was thought 'mad' by some of the men he met. People seem to have taken pity on him for they would some-times give him money or food without his having to beg. Davies's conviction that this suffering was the price he had to pay for success became monomaniacal. Davies wrote about this period about two years later after he had begun to achieve the success he was desper-ate for, but even so some of the intense anxiety and desperate hope of those months reappears in his writing. There is religious fervour in the memory of how he 'worshiped every sabbath night that closed another week' and so brought him closer to his goal. There is desperate conviction in the thought that all his physical sufferings are 'the hard experiences that I was compelled to undergo'. And there is fear of moral derangement in his avoidance of begging on account of the 'strange fascination that arises from success, after a man has once lost his shame' (*AST* 203-7). Davies sounds like a man on the edge of a nervous breakdown, and he may well have been, although if he exaggerated what he endured during these months then his subsequent achievement would have seemed all the greater.

During the second half of 1904 Davies tramped and begged his way down to Devon then back north again to the predominantly working-class railway town of Swindon where he received more charity from working-class people than he usually did in middle-class areas. On the brink of attempting to create a new life for himself as a published poet, Davies seems to have found living an old form of life as a beggar almost unendurable. On reaching Reading he spent a week there, mostly reading in the public library, a brief time he later remembered as showing him how intensely important books were to him. He was planning for the day when the loan from Wales would arrive. He contacted a friend in Canada, one of the officials he met in Renfrew after his accident, and asked him for one pound to be sent by postal order to The Farmhouse. This money arrived in December and he planned to survive for a month on it until the loan arrived in January. He was between two worlds at this time, antici- pating becoming a poet yet having to live as a beggar. In December 1904 he finally returned to London after five months on the road. Although he would have to suffer extreme deprivation living on five shillings a week this was preferable to begging which he could endure no longer, and for which his courage was exhausted. In the first week of January 1905 the loan of thirty pounds came through from Newport. As agreed, Davies would forego all his income during that year. On 12 January Davies arranged for C.A. Watts and Co. of Johnson's Court, Fleet Street, to print two hundred and fifty copies of his volume of poems, entitled *The Soul's Destroyer and Other Poems*, at a cost of nineteen pounds. In the *Autobiography*, at the start of the paragraph relating these events, Davies asserts explicitly one of the book's main ideas that he is a self-made man:

> Now came the new year when, independent of others, I would be enabled to assist myself. If I failed in making success, the dis- appointment would be mine only, and if I succeeded, there would be none other to thank but myself. (*AST* 227)

This is a familiar claim of the romantic artist who thinks that he alone creates himself, that he stands out in this glorious self-creation against an uncaring or even hostile world. The circumstances of this first book's publication, the crucial moment in Davies's career, suggest that Davies was not entirely dependent on his own resources but was being supported. Stonesifer has discovered that Davies was able to show letters of recommendation from two minor critics of the day supporting publication, a fact that Davies failed to mention. And it seems too that the publisher reduced the price asked of Davies towards printing costs (though he did not publish it at his own expense as he later claimed). The volumes were ready in the first week of March 1905, and Davies collected them in three pack- ages, returning with them to The Farmhouse. Watts and Co. had sent out thirty copies to newspapers and journals for review, so Davies's next struggle had begun, the struggle for artistic recognition.

The Soul's Destroyer contained forty poems and was to be sold for 2s 6d. Two lukewarm reviews resulted from the thirty review copies distributed, one in a Yorkshire paper and another in a Scottish one. Reviewers might well have been hard put to make sense of the strange mixture of writing that the book contained. The 'soul's destroyer' of the title poem is drink which kills the man who married a woman loved by the speaker of the poem. Perhaps in discussing all Davies's writing it is appropriate to refer to 'the poet' as the voice of the poems, because although it would be naive to believe that everything that the poems record actually happened to Davies, nevertheless much of it probably did. In many poems Davies no doubt builds up a poem from a fragment of personal experience, but as in the *Autobiography* he also reshapes the experience that may lie behind a poem, or simply invents the whole thing. The title poem, for example, expresses a sense of loss between moving from a life in the Welsh countryside to London, and yet although this may seem simply autobiographical, the city / country contrast is a familiar topic of urban poetry. Davies tries out various literary conventions in this first book. In 'Fortune' he attempts an allegorical argument, with 'Fame', 'Regret', and 'Curiosity' voicing their positions. 'Saints and Lodgers' runs through the names and characteristics of the men in the lodging house, using a catalogue technique that would become familiar from Davies's prose books about tramps and beggars. Other themes appear that would reappear frequently in later poems. Both 'Unholy Meat' and 'The Devil's Guest' express anger at the cruelty meted out to animals by human beings, though the diction and stress may be awkward, as in these lines from 'Unholy Meat':

> Who slays the singing bird, he sins,
>   All other birds he plucks *alive;*
> Who feeds his body from such deed
>   Shall hear of it again, and grieve. (*SD* 26)

The volume shows Davies's weaknesses and his strengths. Strong feelings inform other poems as well as 'Unholy Meat'. 'The Night Walker' is about a woman who makes nightly visits to the gallows where her son is hanging, and the poem celebrates her devotion in the grotesque story of her gathering together her son's body parts as they disintegrate from the gallows:

> And never did thy visits cease
>   Until between the moon and thee
> Thy robber son no more to see,
>   And chain held not one body's piece.
>
>   ...
>
> The proof here in thy house to see –
>   The bones of thy dead robber son,
> Which thou hadst gathered one by one,
>   And thought to bury decently. (*SD* 46)

This unflinching physicality is admirable, as is the emotional directness, probably deriving from Davies's working-class upbringing and his life among the poor. Davies is conscious of the gap between his background and his poetic vocation in 'A Poet's Epitaph', where he remembers his grandmother's prediction that he would just be 'a ne'er-do-well':

> Twas well, maybe, she never heard
>   The rascal call the moon Phœbe. (*SD* 55)

This is awkward too but it touches something real; as does 'Beauty's Light', the first of many poems to celebrate the strong sexual charge in a woman's long hair:

> ... but it is sweet
> Back of that column white as snow
> To let my fingers link and meet
> Under her hair falls, and to know
> Her mine; where it feels warm; a nest
> Just emptied by the birds at rest. (*SD* 49)

This has clichés ('white as snow') but also simple phrases and rhythms that catch sexual feeling ('where it feels warm'); and there is rhythmical deftness in the last three lines. Davies tries to demonstrate his poetic skills in *The Soul's Destroyer* in an impressive range of modes. Ambitious narrative poems jostle with poems of social realism, erotic love poetry with ballads of domestic life. Although the poems may sometimes be technically clumsy, they express original, individual responses to things: grotesqueness, humour, outrage, eroticism, and the banal. Davies does not write like a well-mannered middle-class poet (at least not yet), and much of his originality lies in ignoring those conventions and in treating various subjects, including 'low' ones, with a degree of directness and emotional honesty. The volume as a whole doesn't offer decorous coherence. 'The Devil's Guest' shows the weakness of Davies's writing at this time as its mixed materials fail to hang together: it includes hell where men who vivisected animals are punished, along with a fantasy of chasing a reviewer whose review caused the death of a young poet, and a jocular reference to Davies's wooden leg. Reviewers were more likely to notice the weaknesses of this writing from an unknown poet than respond to its unusual strengths.

In fact reviewers ignored it, and Davies was faced simply with a resounding silence and no income from this book that had cost him so much time and personal suffering to see published. He would receive no income from Wales for seven months, so he was once again virtually destitute and faced with the bitter prospect of going 'on tramp again'. A period of walking the streets and drinking heavily followed. Once again his rage welled up and he considered burning the two hundred copies of the book that he had locked away. But the practical difficulty of burning so many books deterred him. Instead he hatched a plan to raise money by sending a copy of the book to 'successful people' listed in *Who's Who* asking for the two and sixpence that the book was supposed to sell for. The plan required investment in stamps and envelopes, but it began to succeed when some of those solicited sent Davies the money. After a few more weeks Davies had disposed of sixty of his two hundred copies and had some success in 'selling' them. This was an inefficient way of making money, but it made contact with a journalist whose story about Davies would change his life. When success did finally begin to happen it was, Davies wrote, 'all like a dream' (*AST* 232). He was thirty-four years old.

Three: Fledgling Writer and
The Autobiography of a Super-Tramp
1905-1908

Davies sent copies of *The Soul's Destroyer* to eminent people along with a letter requesting payment of two shillings and sixpence. Here is such a letter, couched in humble if not supplicating tones:

> Farmhouse
> Marshalsea Road, S.E.
>
> Dear Sir
>
> I am taking the liberty of sending you a copy of my work. It is very unequal and contains much that I would now gladly withdraw. My motive is to ask you to help me with price of the same, as I am present without means of support. Without troubling you to return the book, and with many apologies for taking this liberty, I remain
> Your humble servant.
>
> William H. Davies.

The letters were mostly met with disregard and uninterest, but when A. St John Adcock, a journalist on the *Daily Mail*, received a copy he saw a story in Davies. Another letter prompted a positive reply from George Bernard Shaw who sent Davies a pound and the practical advice to use the money for postage to send further copies of *The Soul's Destroyer* to a list that he enclosed of eight well-known poetry-loving critics. So Davies sent copies to critics including Edward Garnett, Israel Zangwill, and Edward Thomas. St John Adcock writes of himself in *Gods of Modern Grub Street* that 'being a journalist, he did not miss the significance of this book issuing from a common lodging-house', so he arranged to meet Davies at Finch's

Bar in Bishopsgate Street. Davies showed up but Adcock didn't, and Davies sent a letter on 6 July 1905 which reveals his uncertain, vulnerable state and his precarious financial position. He wrote that he 'had begun to lose confidence', but with letters from Shaw and Arthur Symons he now feels 'assured of my sanity', though he has no idea how his next work is to be published. Another meeting was arranged a few days later in Finch's when Adcock encountered

> a short, sturdy young man, uncommunicative at first, as shy as a squirrel, bright-eyed, soft of speech, and with the general air about him of some woodland creature lost and uneasy in a place of crowds.

Adcock's absurd image of Davies as a shy woodland creature makes Davies seem like some innocent natural rather than the tough man of the world he actually was, though not of the world of literary critics. Adcock won Davies's confidence, and persuaded him to allow an article about him to appear in the *Daily Mail*. This appeared on Saturday 22 July 1905, and in it Adcock told the story of Davies's life as a beggar and tramp. He also gave a critical account of Davies's poems as those of a kind of literary innocent who

> has no pose, makes no excuses for himself, nor appeals for pity, but gives here, in a literary and ethical sense, the best and worst of himself.

According to Adcock, Davies is a simple soul whose personality simply spills on to the page unspoiled by literary sophistication: 'He has a personality', writes Adcock, 'and transfers it to his pages, and that is why ... you cannot fail to be interested in him'. This ignores Davies's considerable literary skills in *The Soul' s Destroyer*, his powers of imitation and experimentation, and it offers a distorting way of seeing Davies's poetry that was often to be repeated in the criticism of him as a good-hearted natural that was to follow. In agreeing to the article in the *Daily Mail* Davies was putting himself at the mercy of a populist newspaper that wanted stories about personalities. Ironically, his big break came not as a result of someone recognising how good his poetry was – Adcock recognised 'crudities and even doggerel in it' as well as 'the freshest and most magical poetry' – but

of someone seeing how his working-class origins, low-life wanderings, and lodging-house life made him a personality. Davies as a poet
was just one element of the larger social oddity that his whole life
constituted. It was as a social freak that he was first displayed to the
respectable lower-middle class readers of the *Daily Mail*.

Attention from other literary journalists immediately followed.
Arthur Symons reviewed what he called 'this curious disconcerting
book' in *Outlook*, and by praising its 'grim directness ... grotesque
humour ... pungent realism' catching something of the volume's
unusual qualities. In the months that followed, *The Bookman*, *The
Athenaeum*, *The Academy*, the *Sunday Chronicle* all suddenly became
interested in this ' tramp poet' and reviewed his book, and *The Tatler*
even photographed him. Davies was deeply excited and disoriented
by all this attention. 'It was all like a dream,' he wrote in the
Autobiography, as one wave of praise succeeded the last, 'for I felt
myself unworthy of it, and of the wonderful sea on which I had
embarked'. Davies became instantly fashionable. Now he received
letters from poetry lovers asking to buy his book, and calls from
ladies wanting to see him and leaving their At Home cards at The
Farmhouse. Davies felt unable to respond to such grand invitations.
According to Adcock's memoirs

> a party of critics, having now bought and read the poems, made
> a pilgrimage to the Farmhouse, and departed to write of the man
> and his poetry (*GMGS* 68).

The newly-fledged poet was temporarily overwhelmed by all this
attention, including, in Stonesifer's words, 'extravagant praise ...
that was not justified'. He was said to be like Thompson, Crabbe,
Wordsworth, and Clare, and declared to be 'a lord of language'. As
Stonesifer puts it, Davies's was a story that was romantic and

> likely to attract attention at that time, for English publishers
> were accustomed to attaching such designations as 'cobbler-
> poet', 'bank-clerk poet', and such like to authors of minor verse.
> (*WHDB* 65)

Davies was a spectacular example of this type of lower-class author,
a publicity phenomenon rather than a recognised poet. He still had

that cultural position to win. Davies's sales improved as a result of the publicity. He wrote to Adcock on 3 August 1905 telling him that his article in the *Daily Mail* had sold twenty-five copies of his poems, and Symons' review had led to twelve more sales, leaving him better off than he had been for a long time, and with about fifty copies still to sell. In August, after a second article in the *Daily Mail* informed the public about the tramp poet's sudden fame, the task of selling copies of *The Soul's Destroyer* was taken out of Davies's hands by the literary agent J.B.H. Pinker who offered to sell the remaining copies at half a guinea each. Pinker began negotiating with a publisher for a second edition of the book, and meanwhile Davies started work on a second collection of poems with help from the lodging house manager, who allowed him to use a room of his to work in, and the manager's wife, who gave him meals. On 13 October 1905 Davies told Adcock that Pinker had only five copies remaining, and mentioned in the same letter that yet another gentleman had called to see him at The Farmhouse, a journalist from the *Daily Chronicle* called Edward Thomas, the man 'who was to do more for him than anyone else' (*WHDB* 68).

Most reactions to the Davies phenomenon expressed middle-class feelings of admiration and wonderment that a man from the working class and a life of destitution could produce poetry, and this often obscured a fair assessment of the book. Davies himself saw the book's weaknesses, and some other reactions were also less starry-eyed. Davies told Adcock that he had 'met queerer people in my correspondence than were ever met personally', and went on,

> One gentleman sends me some beautiful books, his greeting is very friendly and sympathetic, but somehow I can't help being under the impression that he expects something in return.
>
> *WHDB* 66

A strong young man of the working-class had sexual as well as literary attractions for some of his middle-class admirers, and Davies's shrewd tone here reminds us that Davies was worldly, and that Adcock's depiction of him him as a 'woodland creature lost and uneasy' was well wide of the mark. More snobbish was the review in *The Academy* by one Newman Howard whose class feeling is expressed as sneering condescension. 'Someone,' he writes,

> – we are not sure to whom the credit belongs – has excavated
> from far below the Mesozoic Social Strata an object rare always;
> and in its environment unique ... a poet in a doss-house – not
> even a great poet at that.

The sums of what he calls 'our money', he goes on, expended on popular education has resulted only in

> a populace inert, deoxygenised, regaling the grey industrialism
> of their pent lives with comic cuts and the penny novelettes. But
> here at last is a product wholesome and beautiful, however
> slight.

This is the voice of elite culture sneering at a working-class man's effrontery in aping his class and cultural betters. Davies has been made 'vocal only by the aid of elementary education', and is 'the highest articulate product of 300,000 pounds worth of pedagogy' (*WHDB* 67). The nastiness of this is a measure of the snobbery that Davies faced from some people in trying to make his way into the middle-class literary world.

Edward Thomas, however, was a different kind of man altogether. Davies met him on 12 October 1905, and received not only practical help in his literary affairs, but also respect and friendship from Thomas himself along with his wife Helen and children. The two men might have seemed unlikely friends, for both were somewhat reserved and shy, despite enjoying sociability. And even though Thomas's education had been much more extensive and developed than Davies's, they shared common interests in writing about nature. They also had in common their Welsh backgrounds. As R. George Thomas has recorded in his biography of Edward Thomas, the family of Edward Thomas's grandfather had migrated in the early nineteenth century from rural West Glamorgan and Carmarthenshire towards the newly-industrialising towns of Merthyr, Tredegar, Ebbw Vale, Pontypool and Newport (*ETP* 2). Edward Thomas's father had been born in Tredegar, but moved to Swindon when the poet's grandfather took a railway job. There were Newport connections too between Thomas and Davies:

Thomas's mother came from there, and one of her grandfathers, named Marendaz, was a sea captain, like Davies's grandfather. Although Edward Thomas, born and educated in London, was more anglicised than Davies, he would have recognised Davies's cultural background as similar to his own.

Thomas visited Davies before writing his review of *The Soul's Destroyer* for the *Daily Chronicle* to which he regularly contributed reviews. The praise he heaped on Davies's book, along with brief mentions of Davies's extraordinary life, 'must have done a great deal towards making Davies's budding reputation secure' (*WHDB* 69). Thomas wrote that

> to see him is to see a man from whom unskilled labour in America, work in Atlantic cattle boats, and a dire London life, have not taken away the earnestness, the tenderness, or the accent of a typical Monmouthshire man.

Thomas's comment that 'in subtlety he abounds' is perhaps surprising given some of the technical crudities in the collection, but it perhaps suggests one of the personal qualities that drew Thomas to Davies.

Thomas wrote an unusually detailed account of his reactions on first meeting Davies in a notebook headed 'Men'. He took pride in basing his writing on remembered details of conversation, thinking of himself

> as a sounding board for the unrecorded life and language of ordinary people, while reserving for himself the Olympian role of observer and chronicler (*ETP* 127).

The former notion of himself he shared to some extent with Davies, though not the latter. Thomas's notebook entry is worth quoting:

> 11. x. 05. 11.30 p.m. Farmhouse (Harrow St.), Marshalsea Road, S.E. Called and saw William H. Davies author of 'The Soul's Destroyer'. A small narrow-headed blackhaired Monmouthshire man, with the childish slightly uncomfortable smile (with the mouth) of Welsh people, and still a Welsh accent. One leg: the other lost on railway in U.S.A. He is of Maindee near Newport (where Mother lived) and was a picture-framer, but had and has

eight shillings a week left by his sea-captain grandfather, and left Wales ten years ago, and spent five years in U.S.A. and Canada, doing odd work – fruit farming and railways, and then five years in London.

12. x. 05. He showed me his library – Dick's Wordsworth and Shelley; Enfield's 'Speaker', some of Tutin's reprints sent him lately; 2 of St.John Adcock's ditto; and (a recent purchase) a book published last year on 'How to write verse'. I gave him an Oxford Wordsworth in exchange for Dick's – of which the print is cruelly small for a man to read by a coke fire.

Thomas's sharp observation emerges here as well as his practical kindness to this unusual man. The notebook also records something of what Davies offered in return – stories of himself. 'He talked freely and easily with me', Thomas notes,

about early truancy in Tredegar Park – visits to the Ebbw – England v Wales at Swansea five years ago – working his passage across Atlantic eight or nine times in cattle boats.

Apparently warming to his theme, Davies also told him the story about 'Gambling Fred' who claimed that the man who wouldn't lend him sixpence

is now in debt for about £50 (because the sixpence was to go on a horse that won and the fifteen shillings thus made would have gone on another and so on).

This folk tale was just the kind of thing to appeal to Thomas's sense of the authentic.

Edward Thomas made a decisive practical intervention in Davies's life in December 1905. Davies had returned to his mother's house in Newport, 6 Llanwern Street, in October 1905. Buoyed up by the success he had achieved he tried to establish a family home but things did not work out. He first moved with his mother and her family to 1 Woodland Road, a four-storey house with a garden and views from the top room, where Davies started working, over the Usk and the Severn and the new Transporter Bridge. This idyll lasted one week before the landlady promptly asked him to leave. Davies and the family moved to the much smaller house at 42 Dudley Street which was much less conducive to his writing. This attempt at establishing a family life in his home town ended in failure, and is perhaps a sign of Davies's uncertainty about what kind life he might have in the future, now that his long-cherished dream of authorship had been realised. During these disturbed weeks he was planning his autobiography and starting to write it, and keeping in touch with Pinker about bringing out a second edition of *The Soul's Destroyer* and a second volume of poetry. But nothing came of these immediately, and Davies was running out of money and patience. Thomas visited him in Newport in December, and proposed that Davies move to Kent and share a cottage there rent-free from the end of January 1906. Thomas used this cottage as a place to work away from his wife, Helen, and children with whom he lived a few miles away at Elses Farm. When this plan foundered Thomas found another place for Davies. In early February 1906 Davies moved to Stidulph's Cottage, Egg Pie Lane, The Weald, Sevenoaks, the rent of which was paid by Thomas and the cost of coal and light by friends of Thomas's including Edward Garnett. There Davies carried on working on the autobiography, and spent sociable evenings at Elses Farm reading and telling stories to the Thomases (whose daughter Bronwen named him 'Sweet William'), including 'the uninhibited memoirs that appeared later in bowdlerized form'(*ETP* 129). Davies also received intellectual support from Thomas who noticed the inadequate books that he had to read,

> a 6d. Wordsworth and a Shelley ... and one or two strange miscellanies and gifts (of their own works!) from reviewers.

He gave him 'a Wordsworth, a Sturge Moore ... a Byron and a Cowper'(*WHDB* 71).

Edward Thomas was the more intellectually and artistically developed writer when he first met Davies, yet the affinities between them are evident. The first section of Thomas's *The Heart of England* (1906) is described by his biographer as being 'prose poems' that evoke 'moments of perception in natural surroundings'. Davies's poems were very often to do just that too. But Davies was also the sort of man that Thomas was attentive to and would write about – 'vagabonds, tramps, underdogs, and social failures'. Although

Thomas became for a time Davies's patron, he seems not to have patronised him. Rather, he offered practical help by arranging a collection of five pounds from his many friends for Davies, so that when Davies's wooden leg began to splinter, he had a new one made by the local wheelwright, and tactfully commissioned it as a novelty cricket bat; and when the Thomases left Elses Farm, he continued to pay Davies's rent in Stidulph's Cottage. He gave Davies literary patronage too, including publishing examples of Davies's work in *The Pocket Book of Poems and Songs for the Open Air* (1907), and writing to Shaw in late 1907 warning him not to demand excessive terms from Duckworths who might publish Davies's autobiography. When the proofs of Davies's autobiography, published by A.C. Fifield, appeared in October 1907 Thomas corrected them.

Thomas introduced Davies to one London literary circle that met every second Wednesday at the St George vegetarian restaurant in St Martin's Lane. There Davies met Ralph Hodgson, Gordon Bottomley, Arthur Ransome, John Freeman, and Walter de la Mare. Another set of writers, assembled by Edward Garnett and W.H. Hudson, met on Tuesdays at the Mont Blanc restaurant in Gerrard Street, and among those Davies met there were Hilaire Belloc, Ford Hueffer, Walter de la Mare, Norman Douglas, and John Masefield, with John Galsworthy and Joseph Conrad making rare appearances. Davies was thus introduced to the literary scene and quickly gained a wide circle of literary acquaintances and a few literary friends.

Davies must have been writing hard from late October 1905 for he had completed a first draft of his prose autobiography in six weeks. During early 1906 at Stidulph's Cottage he was revising it with advice from Thomas and Garnett, but the process was difficult for him. Writing an autobiography might seem a strange thing for a shy man to do, but the act is complex and what motivates it quite possibly contradictory. As a book about a writer's self an autobiography is self-regarding, even egotistical. The writer's life is worth presenting because the stories and recollections it presents form a plot; it is a life presented as meaningful. And yet in what he wrote Davies seems loath to offer his autobiography as especially meaningful. Its individual stories tend to remain just that, amusing or unusual incidents that do not form a larger significant shape. *The Autobiography of a Super-Tramp* appears to be written as a string of anecdotes recounting the incidents on the surface of an adventurous life. But the genre of autobiography itself pushes the writer towards revealing himself by compelling him to shape his life materials in some way or other. The curious effects that *The Autobiography* produces are explained to a large extent by the tension between conflicting impulses of the author to tell his story while at the same time shielding his inner self, and of the demands of the autobiographical genre, on the other, to tell a meaningful and revealing life story.

In his first draft Davies ignored his years as a tramp in the USA and England and concentrated instead on recounting striking or lurid incidents in his life among the poor and destitute. Davies's first impulse when he began writing the autobiography was to write about sex and drinking, and he would give the Thomases frank accounts of these. He seems to have had little sense of the boundaries of the decent or acceptable that publishers observed in dealing with sexual and possibly violent and criminal material. Perhaps he was genuinely innocent about these proprieties and did not realise that informal censorship prevailed in the publishing world. In any case, Thomas and Garnett inducted him into these, providing detailed advice on cuts, additions and rewritings. Davies was told that some of his material was unpublishable, and though he disliked having to rewrite, reshape and cut his text, he complied. In a letter that Thomas sent to Garnett on 29 August 1905, we get a glimpse of what Davies was going through. 'I am sorry about the Poet's life,' wrote Thomas,

> But I think I have succeeded in setting him to work to increase it as far as possible in the way you suggest. I agree about the details and I think he can do them pretty well. All the additions he has planned are elaborations of episodes hardly touched on before, eg. on tramp in the States and peddling in England; also he himself wished to cut out and mend the London passages. (*WHDB* 74)

The second draft of the book contained no sexually explicit material. What the writing of the first draft and its revision for the second draft suggests about Davies is that to begin with his self-image was located in the narrowly masculine pursuits of sex and drinking. But what the revision also suggests is his willingness to change his self-presentation in order to get published and find readers in respectable literary society. Had he insisted on preserving his sex and drink stories uncensored he would have failed in his attempt to join the ranks of middle-class authorship. He certainly enjoyed talking about his sexual adventures, and according to some of his friends that Stonesifer talked to he would talk about them endlessly unless he were distracted. Conrad Aiken reported rather disapprovingly that 'there had been a lot of sex, and that of the lowest kind'(*WHDB* 94).

Davies's life at Stidulph's Cottage was extremely frugal and lonely, though productive. His regular unearned income of eight shillings a week gave him just enough to live on, with rent, heating, and lighting paid for by Thomas and other supporters. The cottage had a living room on the ground floor and a bedroom on the first floor; and the barest necessities of table, two chairs, camp bed, lamp, and a few pots and pans that came from Edward and Helen Thomas who were themselves not well off. When the weather was cold Davies too was cold in the cottage. But the spring and summer months of 1906 was a happy period when Davies spent time with the Thomases and their children, and walked and talked with Edward Thomas in the Kent countryside. He was continuing to revise the autobiography, and preparing a second volume of poems that would be published in November 1907 as *New Poems*, dedicated to Helen and Edward Thomas. He wrote in its preface that some of its poems were written in London and some in the country. When he showed these poems to Thomas, Thomas was not impressed, and in May 1906 wrote to Gordon Bottomley,

> The Bard is still happy and I think I shall give him a room in my
> next house unless I get a cottage there too. He has shown me 40
> pages of his recent verse and it is painfully mediocre and pas-
> toral, with usually just a faint gleam of original feeling that has
> come through his shabby words – for his style is throughout at
> the level of his poorest in the printed book. It is distressing and
> I have to tell him what I think. (*AS* 35)

When the Thomases had to leave Elses Farm on 26 September 1906 and move to Ashfield, near Petersfield in Kent, they arranged for Davies to continue living in his cottage, but the regular meetings and close familiarity of that summer diminished after they lived further apart.

Thomas continued to advance Davies's career. In June 1906 he arranged for a second edition of *The Soul's Destroyer* to be published by Alston Rivers, which appeared in March 1907, and he helped Davies select from the forty poems of the first edition the fourteen that would constitute the second. In consultation with Garnett, who was a reader for Duckworth which was planning to publish the *Autobiography*, Thomas cast around for someone famous to write a preface to help launch it. Davies wrote to Bernard Shaw asking him to follow up his previous support by writing a preface for his auto-biography. Thomas was thinking ahead should Shaw refuse, and wrote to Garnett suggesting that Arthur Symons or H.W. Nevinson might do instead, though noting that Nevinson's was not a famous name. In the meantime, *New Poems* was published by Elkin Matthews in November 1906 to a muted reception. Thomas wrote to W.H. Hudson when the new book came out, saying that it contained some 'incredibly good' poems, but adding that it was 'not striking like his first' though Hudson would 'like his feeling for nature in the Weald' (*WHDB* 77). He was franker with Gordon Bottomley to whom he wrote asking if he could tell him 'what *favourable* things can be said about it'. Thomas said he would 'think out a just and genial comment for [Davies's] private eye', but in print he would 'praise him mainly because a reviewer has to shout like an actor if he to be heard by the audience'(*AS* 36).

New Poems is an odd mixture of social protest, low life anecdotes, and nature poems. 'The City's Ways' shows how the city is cruel and makes both people and animals suffer, particularly animals driven from the countryside to slaughter in the city:

> Why think of them, though goaded, cursed,
> Of horses, oxen, sheep, in sooth;
> The city's far more hard on men –
> Some starve, some slave, and some do both. (*NewP* 22)

'Wandering Brown' is one of several inconsequential little parables, in this case about a man who once lived in lodging house and now owns a fish shop, that ends oddly:

W.H. DAVIES

'He was a civil sort of cove,
  But did queer things, for one low down:
Oft have I watched him clean his teeth-
  As true as Heaven's above!'cried Brown. (*NewP* 42)

Davies is presumably using scraps of material drawn from his lodging house experiences. 'Saturday Night in the Slums' has considerable force in its raw depiction of urban squalor and violence that Davies sharply registers and recoils from; but 'Whiskey' lapses from social realism into whimsy. Like *The Soul's Destroyer* this second book of poetry experiments with different forms and subjects and attitudes. In the long ambitious poem 'Hope Abandoned' Davies offers an interesting but diffuse mixture of the poet's comments on life in which city and country life are intermingled in an unusual way –

Sweet Nature hath her slums, where crowds
  of flowers
Can thrive, and not make short each other's hours

– and brief moralising comments that add to the original but baffling poetic mixture:

He ceased: he who had fallen in the strife,
And might have sucked some honey out of life
And lodged it in the world's hive to its joy –
But failed, since none would give his brain employ. (*NewP* 75)

When Davies's directness of writing fails him he can sound very like the heroically bad poet William McGonagall. 'The Distinction' is one of the best poems in the collection because its form of alternating iambic tetrameters and trimeters with deftly placed rhymes compels Davies to write pithily and avoid the meandering, unpointed writing of 'Hope Abandoned'. The distinction of the poem is between talent and genius, and the whole poem reads:

This Talent is a slip, or shoot,
  Cut off the family tree;
To train with care and educate,
  Which withers if let be.

But Genius is a seed that comes
>   From where no man doth know;
Though left uncared, aye, hindered too,
>   It cannot help but grow.

Talent's an outlet of Life's stream,
>   Whose waters know no change;
But Genius bringeth in from far
>   New waters, sweet and strange. (*NewP* 15)

Though the metaphor of water in the last stanza doesn't follow from those of the first two stanzas, nevertheless Davies is beginning to produce sharply focused, short lyrics with nicely turned, simple ideas. The difference between talent and genius clearly mattered to him: he appended to his 1923 Foreword to *The Autobiography of a Super-Tramp* a quatrain on the identical pairing, but with a sting in the tail:

Talent gives pence and his reward is gold,
Genius gives gold and gets no more than pence.

The novelty of a tramp poet publishing a book of poems could not be repeated a second time, so now Davies had to win reputation by gaining praise and support for his writing. Critics were lukewarm in their responses to *New Poems* although generally still supportive of the poet in whom they recognised a distinctive voice. In a letter to W.H. Hudson, Edward Thomas picked out as the best poems – mostly short ones that express the poet's responses to nature: 'The Ways of Time', 'Ale', 'The Likeness', 'The Ox', 'The Calm', 'Violet to the Bee', 'Music', 'New-comers', 'Parted', and 'Catherine', poems that are like those Thomas would later write. Thomas wrote three reviews of *New Poems*, the one in *The Bookman* referring with masterly ambiguity to this 'deeply interesting sequel to that first brilliant effort'. He was franker in the *Morning Post* and the *Daily Chronicle*, where he praised the writer as a 'strange, vivid, unlearned, experienced man', and the best of his poems as being those which 'sing themselves through like an old air'. But he criticised 'Hope Abandoned' for its weak construction and obscurity, though even here he managed to praise its being 'rich in more than half-made poetry'. The reviewer in *The Athenaeum* wrote that *New Poems*

> is still a volume of promise rather than fulfilment, but it shows,
> with greater certainty even than *The Soul's Destroyer*, that there
> are possibilities in Mr Davies. (*WHDB* 77)

With the publication of his second volume of poetry Davies showed that at least he could keep going, and reviewers gave him the benefit of the doubt. Thomas even wrote of doing 'what one can to ensure the future of this fascinating genius'(*AS* 37). The book did not sell well; nine months after its publication it had sold only one hundred and sixty copies.

On 6 March 1907 the second edition of *The Soul's Destroyer* was published by Alston Rivers, price one shilling, and it was reviewed by Davies's most determined supporter, Edward Thomas, in *The Bookman* in April of that year. This drastically slimmed-down collection went into a second impression in 1908, a third in 1910, and was reissued again in 1921 by Jonathan Cape, who was by that time Davies's publisher.

None of this did much to relieve Davies's poverty, but Thomas continued to support him financially and act as his unofficial literary agent. In June 1907 George Bernard Shaw wrote a preface for the finally completed version of Davies's autobiography, and the preface and text were sent to Duckworths. Since Shaw now had a part in the book he took it upon himself to insist on some changes to the contract that Duckworth was offering Davies. He challenged Duckworths' exclusive rights to the manuscript in the present and all future editions, suggesting that they be limited to three years. He tried to win Davies a £25 advance and 15% royalties on future sales, and the right to veto any of Duckworths' publicity in order to prevent any 'unusual' publicity that would demean the author. All this contractual wrangling went on over the head of the hapless author who was unused to the roaring of literary lions. Duckworth refused to go along with these demands, but luckily the book was transferred to A.C. Fifield who were presumably more accommodating. Mrs Shaw contributed to the costs of publication with a gift of sixty pounds, and G.B. Shaw suggested the title, *The Autobiography of a Super-Tramp*, by analogy with the title of his successful play *Man and Superman.* The book was published in April 1908.

Shaw's jocular preface buttonholes prospective buyers by its stream of jokes and taunts flying in various directions. Inside this pyrotechnic display, though, is a shrewd assessment of what he calls 'this amazing book'. Shaw does what the journalists who went to The Farmhouse to see the tramp poet did, which is focus on the personality of the author and the peculiarity of his life story, but he makes a literary judgement when he points up the contrast between the roughness of Davies's life and the delicacy of his writing. He warns readers not to expect 'a thrilling realistic romance, or a scandalous chronicle', and signals the author's extraordinary sensibility when he writes that 'these prudent pages are unstained with the frightful language, the debased dialect, of the fictitious proletarians of Mr. Rudyard Kipling and other genteel writers'. Davies is not faking the language of the working-class, as middle-class authors do, but neither is he rendering it realistically, for his characters 'argue with the decorum of Socrates, and narrate in the style of Tacitus'. Shaw's perception is accurate, and he goes on to mention the pleasure the author shows in the book in deploying his language, what Shaw calls his 'scrupulous literary consciousness'. But he then has to make this strange, refined-sounding language of Davies's sound interesting, which he does by more jokes –

> As to the sort of immorality that is most dreaded by schoolmistresses and duennas, there is not a word in the book to suggest that tramps know even what it means.

Shaw treats Davies and his book high-handedly but beneath the banter there lurks his own delicacy and generosity of spirit. He writes how when he first received a copy of *The Soul's Destroyer* his 'imagination failed him' and he 'could not place him'. The begging letter accompanying the book was written in a hand that struck Shaw as being 'remarkably delicate and individual' and the poems themselves contained nothing 'in the least strenuous or modern'; the whole book suggested

> a genuine innocent, writing odds and ends of verse about odds and ends of things, living quite out of the world in which such things are usually done.

Shaw does not see Davies as one of the many types of writer for which there was a vogue in the early years of the century. For him Davies is not simply a working-class or even tramp writer but some kind of original who really does reject work and other social conventions of the middle-class readers whom Shaw is addressing and who will buy the book. In passing, Shaw anticipates another category of readers, namely youths, who would be required to read the book as a school text in years to come. Some of the book's virtues that Shaw touches on – authenticity, simplicity of language, and its masculine focus – would make it attractive in future years to schoolteachers keen to demonstrate to boys that books need not be feminine, and could be safe in the knowledge that it contained nothing sexually explicit.

The neologism 'Super-Tramp' has become a trade-mark for Davies, and as his reputation as a poet has come to depend on a small number of poems regularly anthologised, so his cultural recognition has come to depend more on this memorably titled prose work. When it was published *The Athenaeum*'s reviewer satirically pointed to the gap between the idea of a Super-Tramp – dominant and accomplished in his chosen area – and the figure of the first person narrator of Davies's autobiography,

> a gentleman who makes the old complaint that his minute independent income is the ruin of his life; a weak-kneed 'immoralist' who soothes himself with moral anodynes, and thinks confession good for the soul; a beggar ashamed of begging ... a hawker who 'had neither the courage to beg or sell' ... In fine, the 'Supertramp' is a modest man, of engaging candour, able to give a readable account of himself and the world he has lived in: in every respect the opposite of the 'over-soul' or 'beyond-man'.
>
> (*WHDB* 81)

Shaw's catchpenny title left Davies open to this kind of mockery, and while it may indeed have sold copies and given Davies a higher profile in the literary world, it exacted a price by pinning a label on him that he increasingly came to resent. Davies always thought of himself primarily as a poet who wrote prose from time to time for the income it offered. *The Autobiography of a Super-Tramp*, however, is a skillfully conceived and constructed piece of prose that deserves the praise that Shaw heaped upon it.

Edward Thomas was closely involved in the *Autobiography*'s publication. In March Davies sent him the proofs of the book, hoping that he was not sending them at an awkward time. Any time was awkward for Thomas who was unwell and as usual overworked, but he did the proofreading that Davies was not skilled to do himself. Shaw too was deploying his knowledge of publishing by arranging for his preface and one chapter of the book to be published in the United States in order to protect Davies's and his own copyright. Davies sent Thomas one of the first six copies he received, then celebrated the publication with a bottle of champagne.

The Autobiography of a Super-Tramp is an extraordinary book, as much in the fact that it was published at all as for the stories it tells. The notoriety that briefly stuck to Davies when *The Soul's Destroyer* came out in 1905 revived when he published his own account of his life, but the 'tramp' who emerges from the pages of the *Autobiography* is elusive and individual, not the expected stereotype; and his life story is a strange mixture of elements, not simply 'my life of adventure' as Davies disingenuously presents it. But it was a problem for Davies to know how to present the life of a working-class man with virtually no worldly achievement to his name so as to make it significant and interesting to its predominantly middle-class readers. The book does not describe a rags to riches story; on the contrary, Davies is as poor at the end of the book as he was at its start. And the hero's social trajectory does not trace a success story either; rather it starts in security and ends in insecurity: from his established identity as a boy in tough, working class culture, to his insecurity and humiliation as a one-book poet in the alien literary world. The most striking aspect of Davies's individuality that emerges – a hard core of egotism – both drives his actions and throws into relief the different social worlds through which he moves. Davies himself was not wholly in control of the writing of the book. When he showed the first draft to Thomas and Garnett, they advised him to cut the sexual stories and to add an account of his years in America. Those American chapters amount to almost half of the final version of the autobiography, and contain some of its most interesting sociological and personal material. This suggests that

Davies had no fixed notion of his life's shape and meaning as he was writing and then revising the autobiography. Some of the book's peculiar and unexpected effects may be put down to the way it came to be written, especially its extreme sexual reticence and its narrative jumps and breaks that make its story unpredictable and meandering.

Most of the book is about Davies surviving in the dangerous sub-culture of tramps and beggars. This was his way of life for over twelve years from 1893, yet he presents himself as ill-suited to certain of its demands, and seems never to have become 'completely absorbed into the vagrants' way of life', as Hollingdrake observed (*ST* 17). There is no mention of any fights he was involved in, either as winner or loser, to defend his position in the tramps' social hier-archy, even though he was proud of having been a good fighter as a boy, and makes it clear that the tramps' world operates by a code of individual masculine strength. Indeed he presents himself, far from being a Super-Tramp, as 'an unsuccessful beggar' too sensitive either to demean himself or take advantage of others to be a suc-cessful one. The Davies who emerges from the *Autobiography* is in some ways an outsider to the beggars' world, and even more of an outsider to the literary world at the edge of which he stands facing an uncertain future as the book ends. It is only as a boy in Newport that he describes himself as having a secure place and identity in his culture. So Davies's life story starts from relative boyhood security, moves through adult years of frustration and aimlessness, and ends in change and uncertainty. A very modern story, one might say, with no moral of social advancement, no moment of political or religious conversion, and no sense of an ending.

Davies's values are complex and resist his being stereotyped in any obvious national, class or literary ways. He is, as Shaw noticed, 'a man of independent means – a *rentier*' (*AST* 10) whose tiny private income made becoming a tramp and sustaining that way of life a choice not a necessity. Conventional social respectability is heard several times in the book when, for instance, the phrase 'dirty tramps' prompts Davies to say it is not true physically but 'may be applied morally to them all' (*AST* 172). This thought prompts him to theorise the different kinds of beggars, and this reminds the reader that there are gradations and differentiations enforced among the half-hidden lower strata of society as there are among the respectable and visible. When Davies calls the men gathered at a canal near Chicago 'the riff-raff of America and the scum of Europe', or the transatlantic cattlemen 'the scum of America, a wild, lawless class of people' (*AST* 94, 80), he speaks from his own point of view that in this case is a social and moral superiority over other poor and rootless men. The social world Davies inhabits is itself complex, and the points of view he takes on it are idiosyncratic and inconsistent. This is because he leaves his motives and feelings largely unexamined, and so does not give a consistent account of himself. The phrase 'the old restlessness' is about as much as the reader gets to explain sudden changes of direction (*AST* 99).

He stands slightly outside the world of beggars. The fantasy he secretly harbours is of books and tobacco, and 'a small comfortable room with a cosy fire' where he could read and write (*AST* 59). And he rebukes himself at one point for losing a sense of respectability, and neglecting the cultivation of his mind. These aspirations for material security and high culture obtrude oddly into his account of a vagrant's life. At the same time Davies conceals any involvement he might have had in the criminal activities of beggars (perhaps on Thomas's and Garnett's advice), and he does not admit to sharing the beggars' criminal values. He tells a story of thieving cattlemen stealing from each other on board ship, and admits to stealing a book himself, but says he relents and returns it. The thieves have no honour among themselves, but he does. He is more likely to depict himself as the likely victim of others' crime: travelling to the Klondyke he fears that his travelling companion Three-Fingered Jack will steal his money if he discovers that it's hidden in his money belt. Davies's sense of difference comes partly from the freedom the income from his grandmother's property gives him; from the knowledge that there is always a fall-back should times get too hard for him. This makes his life as a beggar a matter of choice, a fate willingly embraced. He accepts his grandmother's bequeathed income but, although ostensibly rejecting her values, he in fact accepts some of them too, especially those concerning work and respectability. At times he resentfully claims that it was this income that made him 'so idle and so indifferent to saving' and was 'the ruin of [his] life'. This astonishing moment of blaming someone else for his own actions shows how superficial moments of self-awareness in the book can be, and how little they go to explain Davies's actions. The narrator responds to his own obtuseness with a kind of bemused incomprehension:

> 'Ah!' I said, with a sigh, 'if during these five years I had had the daily companionship of good books, instead of all this restless wandering to and fro in a strange land, my mind, at the present hour, might be capable of some little achievement of its own.'(*AST* 120-1).

The narrator seems to be distancing himself from the protagonist here but the effect is incoherent and leaves the reader baffled. While Davies ostentatiously rejects the value of becoming an industrial or a manual worker, he demonstrates an attachment to work even in the *Autobiography* when he spends years in the work of writing. His later life shows him working assiduously at his craft.

The values that Davies is comfortable with are those of working-class south-east Wales: masculinist, home- and family-centred, and patriarchal. The autobiography projects a man's world in which women and what they stand for are almost completely absent. The male protagonist of the autobiography lives by a masculine code of physical courage that is proudly displayed. As a boy he would 'leap over ditches that would try every nerve in [his] body', and in the States he mentions with approval how the 'sheriffs, marshals and constables despise cowardice, and how they respect the intrepidity of dangerous men' (*AST* 22, 65-6). The men living by the canal being dug near Chicago are in danger of their lives from marauding gangs, and of being robbed too. When a man appears who tried to attack the group of men that Davies is part of, he is challenged to a fist-fight by Cockney Tom and after a prolonged bout defeated. Justice is achieved through the code of personal retributive justice, not through the law. The United States section of the *Autobiography* is very like a Western in its characters, narratives and values, and it celebrates a masculine heroism in the face of the risk of death from railroad brakesmen, gangs of murderers and robbers, disease and deadly animals. The struggle is merely to survive, but the consequence for the story is to emphasise moments of exterior action, with no suggestion of the protagonist's inner life or his reflection on what happens. These chapters reach their phantasmagoric climax in Davies's account of nearly dying of fever in a swamp, threatened by hogs and snakes, and drinking stagnant water that 'had the colours of the rainbow, one dose of which would have poisoned some men to death' (*AST* 105). The significance of this episode is its being the ultimate test of manhood; survival against isolation, disease and the natural environment by a solitary man's endurance and courage. No other values are involved and no other people. The moment is supposed to be elemental and universal. But as one critic of the Western has written, the emphasis on the solitary protagonist's facing death so as to prove his courage 'has consequences for the kind of world the Western hero inhabits', for it 'empties the canvas of its details, while placing unnatural emphasis on a few extraordinary moments'. The resulting story 'seems to be telling a universal truth about the human condition' but it 'leaves nearly everything out of account' (*WE* 17). For this reason the narrative in the American chapters is reduced to a string of extraordinary, unrelated moments. The severe limitations of this outlook are demonstrated most sharply and damagingly in the chapter entitled 'A Lynching'.

The lynching that Davies witnesses is described with none of the white racist fury that motivated the lynch-mob's crime. But Davies's code of personal male courage is wholly inadequate to comprehend the terrible scene he is witness to, and perverts his reactions from human sympathy for the man being lynched to anger and contempt at his display of terror, 'screaming, trembling and crying for mercy'. His disgust at the man's display of fear leads him into accepting the position of the white racists who are committing the killing. He remembers newspaper reports of the supposed crime which was 'of the most brutal kind, being much like the work of a wild beast'. This empty formula suggests the prejudice of Southern newspapers against black Americans, especially in the 1890s when lynchings peaked. Black Southerners were blamed by whites for 'the violence that hung over the South', and 'virtually every issue of every Southern newspaper contained an account of black wrongdoing' that fuelled white fears (*PNS* 153). Stories of murder and rape were what aroused white paranoia and sold most newspapers, regardless of whether anything had actually happened. The value of male self-possession by which Davies responds to the lynching, by contrasting the black victim's terror with the white killers' ritualised calm, places the protagonist alongside the murderers. But it also, insidiously, puts the reader alongside the lynch mob too. This is a moment when Davies's unreflective responses are unequal to the scene he witnesses, because they lack the dimensions of historical understanding that would have been needed to comprehend it. Perhaps this is asking too much for a relatively uneducated man who has almost no explicit political perspective on the events he encounters. Davies's reactions are only interesting as another example of how a decent man can easily become a racist. As such it has historical interest. But the racist effect on readers that this chapter has had over the years can only be regretted. The ugliest episode of his time in the South occurs when Davies reaches Paris, Texas, and he is shown the relic of a notorious lynching which happened on 2 February 1893. In a glass case with explanatory printed matter he sees hanging 'something that looked very much like a walnut' which is 'the heart of a negro, whom the people had some-time previously burned at the stake'. Davies, who by this time had been attacked by a gang of blacks and is ready to believe all the stories of black violence he hears, recounts a lurid version of the crime against a 'mere child of a few years, who had been found in the woods torn limb from limb'. The atrocity of the lynching in which the man was burned to death is turned into a story of a woman's justified revenge, as the mother of the murdered child 'applied the torch to this monster', an act, adds Davies, that 'any woman in this land of many millions would have willingly done'(*AST* 111). The actual lynching was a much uglier affair, with the victim's eyes being gouged out with a red hot poker before he was burned to death. Davies not only willingly believes stories of African-American violence but he elaborates the myths with one of his own.

The idea of 'home' is repeatedly invoked in the *Autobiography* as the impossible but desirable dream. What would have consti-tuted a home for Davies, given his mother's remarriage and his own disinclination to follow a conventional life, is unclear. And in fact, when the possibility of returning to Wales offers itself, with enough money saved for the journey, Davies destroys it more than once by blowing the money on what he calls a spree. A summer spent berry picking gives him and Red funds to travel to England but they 'spent it in one week in Chicago, and were again without a cent' (*AST* 73). He is drawn to the idea of the place 'where [he] belonged', but repeatedly avoids a return because the idea is a fantasy. The two attempts he makes to settle once again in Newport fail, the first because he is assailed with his 'fever of restlessness' (*AST* 127); and the second because he and what he calls 'my small family', consisting of his mother and her dependents, are forced by the landlady to leave the house he has just rented. Once this dream proves hopeless, Davies replaces it with another that seems just as unlikely:

> I pictured myself returning home, not with gold nuggets from the far West, but with literary fame, wrested from no less a place than the mighty London. (*AST* 147-8)

Despite being ill-equipped psychologically and materially to realise these family values, and pursuing a way of life in which they are irrelevant, Davies persists in voicing them.

The picture of Davies's relations with women that emerges from the autobiography is falsified by cuts insisted upon by Thomas and Garnett. Only a few coded references to his sex life with prostitutes and poor women remain. When he is in Montreal he learns from an experienced tramp of a place called Joe Beef's where tramps could get a free lunch of beef stew, and soon he hears about French Marie's, 'for these two establishments seemed to be patronised by the same class'. Soon he and his new companion go off for a drink to French Marie's (*AST* 131-2). The nature of French Marie's remains mysterious, and this episode may be a bowdlerised survival of a franker account of Montreal. Davies is certainly capable of slyly hinting at a sexual life. In London, he had dedicated himself to writing, and resolved to give up his comforts of drink, theatres, and 'other indoor entertainments'(*AST* 151). The only women who appear in the narrative as figures with qualities of their own are the matron and her daughter who nurse Davies after his accident. With prostitutes expunged from the narrative the only women who remain are idealised mother figures, for other women are regarded with great suspicion. The members of his boyhood gang warn him against trusting his girlfriend, and sure enough when the boys are caught stealing she and her mother reveal them to the police, proving to him 'even in those early days, how little her sex was to be trusted'(*AST* 24). This is the older man still adhering to his boyhood insight. The only exception to the general rule is his mother whose relationship with her son is mystified. Despite the fact that she had to leave the raising of her children to their grand-parents, and that Davies had had no communication with her for years, he nevertheless represents her relationship with him as one of supernatural sympathy. Returning to Newport unannounced after several years,

> I knocked at the door and mother ... opened the door at once, knew who I was in the dark, though we could not see much of each other's form or face, and, to my surprise, called my by name. 'That's me, mother,' I said. 'Yes,' she answered, 'I thought it was your knock,' just as though I had only been out for an evening's stroll. (*AST* 125)

The dialogue sounds as though it comes from a Victorian melo-drama, but the point is clear: a mother knows her son despite her abandonment of him and his neglect of her. Mystic moments like this do not provide either son or mother with the basis for a renewed relationship, and Davies's several attempts to remake his relationships with family and home all fail. He maintains conven-tional attitudes towards family and home even when actual circumstances might suggest to him that those attitudes can never be realised by him or his family. His lack of self-reflection stops him from seeing how much his values have been altered by his wander-ing life. In many respects the *Autobiography* is the story of a conventional man living an unconventional life, and perhaps the book's attachment to conventional values made it popular when it was first published and for many years afterwards.

Helen Thomas read the autobiography and declared it to be 'the work of a genius of rare power', the first of many enthusiastic responses to it. Edward Thomas wrote two positive reviews, continuing to support Davies's literary career. And indeed the *Autobiography* did bring Davies back to the public's attention with a book that achieved good sales immediately, and continued to sell. Fifield brought out a second edition in 1908 and a third in 1911. An American edition of ten thousand copies was published by Knopf in 1917, with a second edition in 1925. In Britain the book has been almost uninterruptedly in print since its first publication. According to Stonesifer, this book gave Davies 'a steady if tiny source of income through the years' (*WHDB* 81). In 1908, however, Davies experienced little change in his financial circumstances, and he commented ruefully on his continuing poverty going along with increased fame. The rent of his cottage was still being paid by Thomas, and he was living there alone, reading and writing, and working on his next volume of poetry. This way of life suited him, according to his biographer, for 'deep within him was a very real fear of personal entanglement' (*WHDB* 82).

Four: Edward Thomas and the Professional Writer 1908-1914

Securely ensconced in his cottage in The Weald, Davies's fantasy of a cosy room with books and time to write – a fantasy unrelated to that of 'family' – was virtually realised. It suited him well, and his literary output during the decade after he moved to The Weald in 1906 was considerable. He published eleven books between 1907 and 1914.

The friendship between Edward Thomas and William Davies continued to flourish. Thomas supported Davies financially and offered him what Davies obviously considered essential advice and guidance on his work as it progressed, and on navigating the treacherous waters of literary London. In May 1908 Davies sent Thomas poems that would appear in *Nature Poems* asking if he 'could glance at them, and mark what you approve of, at your leisure'. Davies was shrewd enough to realise that the success of the *Autobiography* created favourable conditions for launching a new book of poems, and he happily took any opportunities that offered themselves for publicising either himself or his poetry. In May 1908 he was photographed for an article on tramps for *The Idler*, and then sent them three or four poems for publication even though, as he told Thomas, 'the *Idler* only pays five shillings for a poem' (*AS* 43-4). Thomas reviewed the *Autobiography* in the *Daily Chronicle* and the *Morning Post*, with lavish praise and acuity. He noticed that the narrative depended on Davies's egotism, on what was 'of first-rate importance to himself', and claimed that the clarity of its style flowed from Davies's 'strength and simplicity and nonchalant grasp of life'. He recommended it as 'a sociological document ... of the life of tramps in England and America', and defined the literary type to which it belonged as 'picaresque romance'. Davies was pleased with this praise, and wrote to Thomas that his reviews 'had been the best which, of course, I quite expected' (*AS* 43). The friendship between the two men was important to Thomas too who visited Davies regularly in his cottage and with whom he felt in sympathy. For Thomas literary and personal sympathies combined, for part of his literary ambition was to find a way of expressing what his biographer calls 'country scenes and country people [along with] his own specialized insight' (*ETP* 131), and Davies seemed to offer him one version of the experience of ordinary people and the natural world, and one way of trying to express it. When Thomas was feeling low about his writing, Davies was one of the friends, along with Edward Garnett, James Guthrie and Walter de la Mare, who 'strengthened [his] determination to continue with his own, financially unprofitable writing experiments' (*ETP* 163). Perhaps too there was an affinity between the friends in that part of their personalities that harboured intense feeling. Thomas was capable of being driven to excesses by his temperament: Davies was a man in whom lay powerful, at times overwhelming feeling, and who expressed it occasionally in extreme actions.

Davies was reading and writing during this period. While tramping on the road in England he had carried with him a bible and a cheap edition of Wordsworth. In Kent he read widely, going to Sevenoaks Library for half an hour every morning at one time, and receiving books from Thomas, including an edition of Walt Whitman in October 1909. He read English sixteenth- and seventeenth-century lyric poetry, and drew from that source much of his poetic manner. In October 1908 A.C. Fifield published his *Nature Poems*, the volume that established unequivocally his standing as an accomplished poet who could speak to his times. There's a note of relief as well as admiration in a letter that Thomas sent to Gordon Bottomley on the publication of this book: 'O yes isn't Davies fine now?'. Thomas's faith in the unlikely author, his support for him even when Davies's writing was disappointing or in need of revision, was fully vindicated. 'I was terribly excited over the new book,' he went on, 'It was almost incredibly good' (*AS* 45). The lyric quality of this collection owed much to Davies's ease at living at the Elses Farm cottage. His biographer thinks that writing the

Autobiography had 'served to release his spirit' and helped him control memories of the past. And Davies himself recalled in *Nature* how living in 'these pleasant conditions' he was 'in the mind to give all [his] thoughts to Nature'. His outlook at this time was deter-minedly optimistic: 'There were to be no weeds, but all flowers' (*WHDB* 84), and this sunny outlook is reflected in the 1908 volume that resulted.

Although Thomas reported rather ironically that 'Yeats wants him to "cultivate his instrument" more' – presumably his poetic skills – and added, 'But Davies wouldn't know what the phrase meant' (*AS* 45), *Nature Poems* does in fact display a widened range of poetic skill. There are different kinds of poems (allegorical, narra-tive, lyric), and a variety of forms and feelings on show. While Davies's subject and outlook may have narrowed to nature and the optimistic, his poetic technique is increasing in range. Some themes are familiar from his first two books of poetry: memories or antici-pations of physical love are represented in a curious range of images. The love poem to 'Jenny' suggests fierce sexual response,

> You'd think if passion stirred her she
>   Could bite and hurt a man of stone.

as well as Medusa-like dangers:

> Her curls, like golden snakes, would lie
>   Upon each shoulder's front, as though
> To guard her face on either side ... (*NP* 13)

Davies's fascination with the lure of women's hair is also expressed in 'A Maiden and her Hair' where the girl's hands are

> Tossing the loose hair to and fro,
>   Until, like tamed snakes, the coils
> Lie on her bosom in a row.

'Love's Birth' suggests a distinctly modern love psychology, a mixture of possessiveness, paranoia, domination, and distance:

> I heard one day a step; a voice,
>   Heard in a room next door to mine;

And then, I heard long, laughing peals,
    For *him*! from Rosaline.

Again she laughs; what, mocking me?
    I shook like a coward in the night –
Who fears to either lie in dark
    Or rise to make a light.

For weeks I cursed the day I met
    That fair sleep-robber, Rosaline;
Till Love came pure from smoke and flame –
    I swore she should be mine.

And in her house I held her firm,
    She closed her eyes and lay at rest;
But still she laughed, as if a bird
    Should sing in its warm nest. (*NatP* 32)

It is difficult to say if the woman here becomes desirable because she is being enjoyed by another man or because of her disturbing laughter, but even after she is enjoyed, she remains elusive. This is more emotionally complex than anything that Davies had attempted before. The image of a warm of nest has become one of Davies's motifs for intimate sensuality. Davies's poetry is conventional in many ways, especially in its form and range of subject matter, but he regularly gives a fresh twist to familiar subjects that revivifies them. He adopts a range of poetic voices, such as the 'jolly' speaker of 'A Beggar's Life', celebrating how he can 'do no work and get my need', and smugly enjoying his idleness and the favours of other men's wives:

When farmers sweat and toil at ploughs,
    The wives give me cool milk and sweet;
When merchants in their office brood,
    Their ladies give me cakes to eat,
And hot tea for my happy blood;
    This is a jolly life indeed,
    To do no work and get my need. (*NatP* 19)

The tone of 'A Lovely Woman' is ardent to the woman, and sardonic to other men who like the speaker are also drawn to her; and here the half-rhymes and varied four-stress line give the sense of a mind in motion:

> A woman moving gracefully,
> With golden hair enough for three,
> Which, mercifully! is not loose,
> But lies in coils to her head close;
> With lovely eyes, so dark and blue,
> So deep, so warm, they burn me through.
> I see men follow her, as though
> Their homes were where her steps should go. (*NatP* 46)

Despite his growing poetic skills, Davies's language still registers attitudes and perceptions that spring from his working-class background and from a personal outlook unconstrained by educated, middle-class decorum. This sometimes appears in extraordinarily physical metaphors, as when a girl runs her fingers through her hair – 'Her cruel hands go in and out, / Like two pale woodmen working there' ('A Maiden and her Hair' *NatP* 16); or when a woman's falseness is discovered, 'I found thee false, thy looks deceived / Like short men that sit tall' ('Vain Beauty' *NatP* 58). Increasing poetic skills did not involve the abandonment of the bold modes of representation of the primitive artist.

It was not only Edward Thomas who was enthusiastic about this new book. Arnold Bennett called it 'indubitably wondrous', and gushed, 'I won't say that it contains some of the most lyrical lyrics in English, but I will say that there are lyrics in it as good as have been produced by anybody at all in the present century', though perhaps that was not such a large claim to make in 1909 (*WHDB* 84). Probably Bennett was right to identify Davies's lyrics as the best poems in *Nature Poems*. The longer poems are overstretched, like 'Waiting', or bombastic like 'A Familiar Voice' which hymns Wales in sentimental terms: 'For Wales is Wales; one patriotic flame / From North to South, from East to West the same' (*NatP* 35). The best poems are short, romantic nature or love lyrics, and through these Davies was fashioning himself, and being recognised by critics, as a kind of romantic nature poet. Davies's solitary life continued in writing and reading in his library of fifty or so books, including Shakespeare, Milton, Wordsworth, Byron, Burns, Shelley, Keats, Coleridge, Blake and

Herrick. Oddly, he now claimed that after years of having to make do with books borrowed from public libraries, he only enjoyed books that were his own possessions: 'I want to see the books around me as my own property, else the sight of them grieves me' (*WHDB* 86). He began sending individual poems to magazines and periodicals in the hope of generating a regular income to improve his still shaky financial state, a matter on which Edward Thomas once again gave him advice. Davies regarded magazines with suspicion, complaining to Thomas that the *Nation* was holding on to some of his poems too long. In December 1908 he managed to get a piece published in the *English Review* on 'How it feels to be out of work', which is not so much about what the title suggests but rather how a working man can become a beggar by seeing the good life beggars enjoy, and so come to enjoy 'the air of freedom' himself. It's a subversive little piece, part fantasy, part sociology, that ends with Davies expressing amusement at how busy men 'are always trying with all their might to make up the time they wasted as babes in their mothers' arms, and in idle play in fields and streets' (171). He was writing other essays on begging, and circulating them for publication without much success; but his writing was assiduous and his commitment to his life as a writer total. The only interruption occurred in July 1909 when he had to move from Stidulph's Cottage, because the farmer needed it for a farm worker, and Davies became a boarder in a house in Sevenoaks.

In September 1909 his prose work *Beggars* was published by Duckworth, and was favourably received. The *Liverpool Courier* said it was 'sociologically of great value', and the *Irish Times* reviewer thought it would 'become a classic on the subject'; and indeed it is still read at the end of the twentieth century for what it records of beggars' lives at its start (*WHDB* 89). The book also showed Davies's considerable skill as a prose writer. Thomas, in a review in the *Morning Post* in October 1909, praised the 'purity and simplicity' of the book's style, and thought it was 'more subtle and various ... than the *Autobiography*' because Davies's 'powers of reflection and criticism have increased'. He still saw Davies as a kind of artistic innocent, however, insisting that his stylistic powers 'are doubled in their effectiveness because he is unaware of them' (*AS* 46). This view of Davies as untutored and naive was becoming established, and was to become in the years to follow the familiar way of accounting for him. Despite Davies's aspiration to artistic equality with other writers of the present and past, he came to be seen as a kind of artistic freak of nature, a simple soul with a large but naive creative gift. In fact the stylistic accomplishment of this writing was as much the product of his determined self-education and his application to writing as it was to natural powers. *Beggars*, and other prose works such as *A Poet's Pilgrimage*, base their technique on the working-class oral storytelling that Davies was exposed to from his earliest years in his grandfather's pub, and among beggars and working people. Davies is an accomplished exponent of that oral storytelling style, but his skill in that discourse is invisible to middle-class critics. They represent it as an unconscious natural power. The literary agent Thomas Burke writes of Davies in his memoirs that 'nothing he writes comes from brain or study', and that 'he writes a poem, as other men shave', presumably unthinkingly. Instead of seeing Davies in terms of his complex social history, he mystifies him by turning him into an inspired animal: Davies's face shines with a light 'that comes from something higher than intellect', and his eyes are 'large and deep and brown and placid; they belong to the horse or the deer' (*CE* 88-9). Despite Davies's efforts to have himself taken seriously as a poet, his image as man emerging from the social depths was preserved by the publication of such books as *Beggars* that repeatedly reminded the reading public of 'the tramp poet' and his strange emergence from obscurity.

Beggars resembles those chapter of *The Autobiography of a Super-Tramp* which abandon narrative and focus on a subject (such as 'Gridling' or 'Rain and Poverty'), or tell a self-contained story (like 'The Fortune'). The writer as subject drops out of view and we have only a loosely strung set of stories, memories, reflections and observations from Davies's years in the United States and London. Written from the depths of the English rural south about a past life, his view of beggars is fairly detached and ironic. Of Welsh beggars, for instance:

> I have only met about half a dozen in America, and they were so timid that Wales had as little cause to be proud of them as Ireland

of hers. I don't think Welshmen take kindly to begging, for, according to my later experience at home, half the beggars in Wales are Englishmen, though many of them can explain themselves in Welsh, having been in the country a considerable time.

His is a back-handed compliment to himself and his countrymen, of course; and his nation too is praised, 'for Wales runs America a good second in her generosity to beggars' (B 8-9). What we hear in such passages are the well-worn stories of a good talker, shaped and polished and very much on their best behaviour. Polite language prevails here as it did in the autobiography, with 'gol darn' being the nearest it comes to swearing. Despite the reticent language, Davies deals frankly with the violence of vagrants' lives. The chapter about the violence of gangs of boys analyses precisely how and why it is so dangerous: 'when a number of these half boys and half men are together, they want sport and romance as well [as robbery]'. It is these 'young bullies' that 'make the slums of London and other large cities so dangerous', for 'they obey the first impulse, which, more often than not, is a cruel one; and the cruelty increases with their strength of number'. When a gang of them meets a drunk man, the 'one of them steps forward and sometimes to disguise his intention, holds out the hand of friendship, and the poor drunkard receives a blow in the face instead'; and, if he tries to fight, they 'will all try their strength on him and probably leave him insensible in the gutter' (B 83-85). First-hand knowledge gives these pages their authenticity and force. In the yarns about low life it is the simplicity of style (as Thomas called it) that catches and holds the reader's attention. This is difficult to demonstrate with a short quotation, but the following extract gives some sense of Davies's storytelling skill. He has just tried and failed to beg money from a gentleman by telling him his story:

> In five minutes after I was hailed by a voice from the hedgerow, and, looking in that direction, saw the most ragged man I had ever set eyes on, with his matted hair a foot long. 'Did you meet a gentleman on your way?' he asked. 'I did,' said I; 'and what of that?' 'That man,' said the ragged tramp, 'was a thoroughbred. He saw me sitting here and, without a word from either of us, he emptied his pocket into my hand' – saying which he with-

drew his fingers from the palm of his hand and disclosed to my view three pennies. Now, here was a workhouse tramp – for he was no other, or he would at once have stepped into the road and accosted the gentlemen – receiving unsolicited alms; and I, who earned my living by the use of my tongue, must suffer in consequence. (*B* 124-5)

This is almost Shavian in its shifting ironic tones, and shows the humour that Thomas found in the book. Davies can write in these various ways because he is free from the need to tell the story of himself, as he has to do in *Autobiography of a Super-Tramp*. In *Beggars* he can simply use his store of experience and his storytelling skills to produce a constantly changing kind of writing that keeps on being interesting and entertaining.

Davies was writing poems for his next collection, *Farewell to Poesy*, that was published by Fifield in 1910. By this time he was a client of the literary agency run by Frank Cazenove, who dealt with the authors, and G.H. Perris, the business brains of the operation. Cazenove was a man who recognised literary value and was pre-pared to support it, as he did in the case of Edward Thomas for whom 'he worked for years at a return which scarcely covered his postage costs in their correspondence' because he recognised him as an artist (*CE* 79). A story told about Cazenove suggests that he was well able to recognise the storytelling skills of a book like *Beggars*. He told his assistant to study the construction of the dirty story, 'They've got to be short to hold the listener,' he told the young man, 'and it's got to be all there. All the art of the short story is to be found in the unprintable ones – precision, economy, interest and finish' (*CE* 79). Cazenove acted in Davies's interest by sending his poems to various periodicals, though Davies was often dissatisfied at the careless way he felt periodical editors treated his work. He was annoyed when the *Nation* lost two of the dozen prose sketches he had sent them along with a dozen poems. Nevertheless, poems that found their way into *Farewell to Poesy* were first published in the *Nation* and *Country Life*. This provided a trickle of income, and along with the substantial royalties he was receiving from the *Autobiography*, and the smaller amounts from *Nature Poems*, it gave him enough money by the summer of 1909 to free Thomas and other supporters from paying his rent and expenses, and to start paying his own rent.

Sevenoaks was congenial in some respects though not in all. Davies made friends, and a number of names crop up in his letters to Thomas. Perhaps genteel Sevenoaks provided him with experience of dealing with the middle classes that would be useful when he made contact in London with the upper-middle and upper classes. He received a written invitation to tea from a Mrs Podmore, 'a lady'. The local manager of Lloyd's Bank accepted Davies as a customer when he received Edward Thomas's name as a reference. Regular friends named in Davies's letters included a Mr Seamur, a broad minded religious man who did 'not force religion down people's throats', and Mrs Graham, who together with Seamur planned to start a branch of the Poetry Recital Society in the town. Davies rambled with Jones and Hooton, and with Thomas when he appeared in the area. Other rambling friends included W.L. Anckorn who remembered Davies as a solitary man who found it difficult to make friends because he had very little small talk. 'Only to his closest friends,' Anckorn recalls, 'would he talk about his work' (*WHDB* 90). There were two men who were socialists, with whom Davies become friendly, Arthur Hickmott and Herbert Cole. They were both members of the Independent Labour Party. Cole was an artist, and Hickmott a poet, and along with Davies they enjoyed politically challenging and culturally informed conversation. They provided Davies with 'companionship and stimulus that he had received only on his infrequent trips to London' (*WHDB* 90).

Social life in Sevenoaks, however, also produced its anxieties for Davies. After he had been to the Littles for tea, who were 'very nice people', he wrote to Thomas asking, 'what would be the best time to call on them again, so as not to call at meal times' (*AS* 50). The social scene in Sevenoaks all sounds like something from an E.M. Forster novel. Wealthy businessmen who worked in London lived there, and Davies realised that, if they knew of him at all, they would regard him with suspicion or contempt. Stonesifer tells how Davies took the opportunity of a poetry reading to express his antagonism towards the locals. He read Browning's 'Soliloquy of the Spanish Cloister', and when he reached the last line, 'Gr-r-r – you swine!', he delivered it directly and feelingly to his audience.

Farewell to Poesy was published at one shilling in February 1910, only five months after the publication of *Beggars*. The poet's point of view in this volume is complex: he remembers the squalor and suffering in the city at the same time as responding strongly to his country surroundings. Memories of the doss house mingle with reactions to nature in 'Now'. 'In the Country' reflects on his intense enjoyment of country life as 'a selfish thing' because it avoids 'the human suffering' of 'poor creatures' (*FP* 24) in the city, and yet the poet is helpless to relieve it. The poet is morally sensitive to the conflicts his own escape from degraded living conditions has brought about. In 'Selfish Hearts' the misery of 'the working mass' is compared with the selfishness of the rich and, interestingly, with beggars who beg 'With selfish heart' (*FP* 17-18). It seems that Davies's experience of Sevenoaks may have sharpened his sense of the unfairness of society. As an ex-beggar he identifies neither with working men nor the well-off, even though beggars live a life of social irresponsibility like many of the wealthy and are often destitute like many workers. Another poem expresses the contempt for respectable values from the beggar, whose

> ... lips do whine, but how his heart doth laugh!
> To think that he is free to roam at will,
> While others toil to keep that thing 'Respect'
> > ('The Philosophical Beggar' 42-3).

Davies writes on some of his by now familiar themes in this book. His hatred of animals enduring cruelty from humans is expressed in a telling phrase in 'The Dumb World', 'A dumb thing near a drunken man' (*FP* 20). His fascination with the erotic power of women appears in poems that detail, in franker and more subtle ways than earlier poems, the entanglement of eroticism in everyday life, and its perversities. 'On Expecting Some Books' dwells on the comforting sensuality of books, and contrasts their quiet dependability with women's sulks and jealousies, and their subjecting men to control and surveillance:

> When
> I'm visited by living men,

> They will not sulk and cast black looks
> When left unflattered ...
> The one in leather will not chide
> To feel a cloth one touch his side. (*FP* 32)

'Hungry' touches on sadomasochistic feelings when the poet details how he is aroused by his lover's red-faced anger, depicted in the extraordinary image, 'her face flogged by / The wings of Butterflies' *FP* 35). 'To a Flirt' expresses the poet's anger at a woman perversely flirting with him in order to arouse another man's sexual interest in her:

> You'll get no help from me,
>   To make him prove,
> With jealous looks and words,
>   His backward love. (*FP* 31)

Some of Davies's subjects and attitudes in this volume may well have been modern but some of his styles were drawn from old models. The Wordsworth of the *Lyrical Ballads* lies behind 'Old Ragan', the story of a rural hermit and misanthrope; while Keats is the model for the heavy poeticisms of 'The Kingfisher'. Davies's imitations of Romantic voices, though they are often merely conventional, were a part of his extending technical expertise. Poems that catch something of Davies's modernity in demotic language are usually his best, most characteristic writing. This collection shows him continuing to experiment with styles and subjects, and achieving distinctive effects by bringing together his idiosyncratic view of things with robust language. 'An Old House in London' is a fantasy of an old house in Southwark reimagined in its original rural setting. Its original bucolic existence provides a critique of the present squalor and the poverty of its inhabitants:

> In fancy I can see thee stand
> Again in the green meadow-land;
> As in thine infancy, long past,
> When Southwark was a lovely waste;
> And Larks and Blackbirds sang around...
>   We see no more
> Green lanes, but alleys dark instead;

Where none can walk but fear to tread
On babes that crawl in dirt and slime. (*FP* 25-6)

Davies's originality carries risks of bathos and grotesquerie, of course, but they are an effect of the same will to individual expression. In 'Now', it is uncertain if the metaphor of men sitting round a dangerous coke fire 'Like frogs on logs' is grotesque humour meant to intensify the horror or just ill-considered. Davies can certainly write in a way that combines grotesque language and banality to produce unsettling effects, as in 'Old Ragan':

He throws his fowls their own eggshells,
  Feeds them on thrice-boiled leaves of tea;
And dead flies on his window-sill,
  He killed when they danced merrily. (*FP* 30)

Davies was pleased with the critical reaction to *Farewell to Poesy*, writing to Thomas that Shaw thought it his best work and a 'distinct advance on the others'. In the meantime he was busy writing a novel that was completed by autumn 1910 and was to appear in February 1911 entitled *A Weak Woman*. The ever-generous Thomas helped Davies with the proofs as did Edward Garnett, but even their suggestions could not give this prose a sense of being fiction. Davies was writing indefatigably at this time, as his string of publications testifies: *Songs of Joy*, another poetry volume, came out in November 1911, *The True Traveller*, more prose reminiscences of his tramping experiences, was published in March 1912, and *Foliage*, more poems, in September 1913. This period of his life from 1906 to 1913 while he was living in and around Sevenoaks has been described by Hockey as 'his greatest period' in which 'Davies had laid the sure foundations of his literary career' (*WHD* 55). The period ended with the publication of *Foliage* and Davies's moving to London, and he was never to be so prolific again. Davies's financial position was transformed by the award to him in July 1911 of a Civil List pension of fifty pounds per year. Edward Thomas had organised a petition, then written to the prime minister, Asquith, and won his approval for the idea. He enlisted Ernest Rhys, the distinguished Welsh publisher working in London, telling him that Davies was 'on the rocks', and together they went to the House of Commons to win the support of some Welsh MPs. Rhys's account of their visit in his memoirs gives a sense of the small establishment world that operated by personal contact and recommendation, and how it was necessary to please them in order to win favour:

> We met at Charing Cross, and as Davies limped up in the crowd he looked like a countryman in town for a holiday, dressed in a worn grey suit, with a short pipe in his mouth and a cloth cap on his head. Neither Edward Thomas or I wore anything like town clothes, and together we made as queer a trio as ever went to lobby an M.P. at the House. We had our eye upon a man after our own fancy, Llewellyn Williams, then member for Carmarthenshire. Himself a writer of good stories and a bit of a poet and history man, he had edited some volumes of Froude for me in Everyman's Library. He looked like a mixture of a jolly Welsh farmer and a judge ... In short, the one man in the House to understand W. H. Davies. He gave us tea in the smoking-room, and regaled us with toasted buns and droll stories, and our mirth grew so loud that the other members in the room looked uneasy. Our mission was quite successful. True, it was not a big pension to begin with, but it was enough to get the poet on his way. (*WEW* 170-71)

The pension, later increased to £100 then £150, provided Davies with security for the rest of his life. Thomas's earlier attempt to see Davies financially secure by getting him a sinecure in the British Museum was indignantly refused. Davies's friend Richard Church reported years later how Davies reacted to the offer of this 'nice little job': 'they expected me to work. I have never worked in my life. That's what your friends do for you!' Luckily he had friends who were willing to go to great trouble on his behalf to help him avoid the horrors of regular work. In the first half of 1911 Edward Garnett was working to obtain Davies a grant from the Royal Literary Fund, which he succeeded in doing. It is no coincidence that Davies's next book of poems was called *Songs of Joy*. In May 1911 he went off for a number of weeks tramping, something he did from time to time, and when he was, as Stonesifer says, 'hardly distinguishable from the tramp he had formerly been' (*WHDB* 93). The experiences he had during these wanderings provided him with fresh material to include in his prose books about tramps. Poetry provided little steady income, but his reputation as the 'Super-Tramp' continued to interest the public enough to support the publication of more tramp books from Davies. *The True Traveller* of March 1912 is extraordinarily interesting for its sexual frankness as well as its smooth technique. Davies's shrewd sense of the reading public's preferences prompted him to make the most of his reputation and experience and turn them into marketable books, though he would have preferred simply to have written poetry. He wanted to be thought of as a poet but he showed as much literary skill as a raconteur.

Songs of Joy confirms Shaw's judgement of the previous book of poems that it indicated a distinct advance technically and in its subjects. Davies's poetic forms here include 2-stress lines ('The Winged Flower'), 3-stress ('Man'), as well as complex poetic forms that show George Herbert's influence ('The Posts'):

> A year's a post, on which
> > It saith
> The distance – growing less –
> > To Death. (*SJ* 42)

Davies also imitates Shakespeare's 'Blow, blow thou winter wind' from *Twelfth Night* in 'Love's Happiness', suggesting a growing confidence:

> Blow, blow, thou Eastern wind,
> > Since Love can draw thy sting;
> The South blows to my mind
> > And does sweet odours bring –
> If only Love is kind. (*SJ* 57)

He also seems to have been reading Marlowe's *Dr Faustus* for Faustus's enthralled speech to Helen is echoed in 'Love's Power':

> Thy touch can launch a fleet of boats
> Sunk to their decks with bales of bliss,
> To take the tide of my blood-veins
> Straight to my Heart's Metropolis. (*SJ* 16)

This is a more complex use of metaphor that overlays boats navigating the sea with flows of blood and feeling in the body.

The title of the book is apt for it contains energetic, ardent, purposeful writing; and the joys it refers to are singing and drinking, the sexual attractions of women, and various kinds of free living. In 'The Bed-sitting room' the poet spurns a landlady's room that threatens a free life:

> What then? I think this life a joyful thing,
> And, like a bird that sees a sleeping cat,
> I leave with haste your death-preparing room. (*SJ* 86)

The sharp political sense glimpsed in *Farewell to Poesy* appears explicitly here in 'To a Working Man' who is urged to 'meet your masters in debate: / Go home from work and think and read – / To make our laws is your true fate' (*SJ* 25). Also becoming more developed is Davies's erotic writing, which previously was often directed towards undifferentiated women or their body parts, but in this volume is worked into more complex relationships. 'To a Rich Lady' sets wealth and its social life against the elemental nature of sex, for even though the woman has 'rooms to spare' and 'friends' that 'come and go', 'Still would I ask for no more space / Than where two bodies could embrace' (*SJ* 61). Sex is valued more highly than social privilege; it is another of life's 'joys' that critiques conventional values. The poet's fantasised power is in having sex to offer the rich lady, but also in having to 'ask' her for it. This is the eroticisation of begging that can also be seen in some of his begging tales. Other poems openly express unrespectable sexual feelings. In 'A Dream' a man meets a woman in a wood, goes to her cave to make love to 'That fair Enchantress', and there enjoys the ferocity of her love-making as he discovers that 'Her teeth are made to bite / The man she gives her passion to' (*SJ* 66). In 'The Power of Music' male passivity is imagined as well as the intensest pleasure that music can create:

> Do with me, O sweet music, as thou wilt,
> I am thy slave to either laugh or weep. (*SJ* 37)

This increased sexual frankness was no doubt a sign of the times, as writers pushed back the limits of what could appear in print. But for Davies there were particular reasons. For one thing, while he was writing the poems in this collection he was also writing *The True*

Traveller which included a good deal of material about his experiences with prostitutes. For another, in 1910 Edward Thomas was working on *The Feminine Influence on the Poets* and was trying to discover 'as many different ways as possible of establishing a relation between "reality" and a poem to or about an individual woman'. He wrote to a number of friends, including Davies, asking them for 'the circumstances under which [a particular poem] was written and what relation it bears to "reality", *if any*'. Davies's response of 15 April 1910 was enthusiastic about the project, and gave Thomas details of the experiences that lay behind several poems; along with his general rule that 'I never write a love poem but that I have some real woman in my mind; either one I have met in the past or one I meet now, and whose looks I like' (*AS* 53). Davies thought of himself as a lover, a notion that owed a good deal to the poetry he had read and which was then acted out in his life; and it involved acute responsiveness to the ways that girls and young women looked and acted: the 'sweetest laugh' of one, the singing of another, or 'the looks' of a third. As a lover he retains these fragments of memory, but he is also bold and skillful in pursuit. The woman who affected him most, he told Thomas,

> was one I met on the Thames Embankment, whom I had never met before, and have not seen since. I followed her about for a considerable time, and noticed that everyone, no matter of what age or station in life, stared hard at her. Her own apparent indifference gave them a good chance to do this. It was with much disappointment that I at last came to the conclusion that she had nothing to do with men, and let her pass out of sight. (*AS* 53)

Davies was proud of himself for being what he called a 'real lover', and compared himself favourably with Wordsworth in this respect, who 'would have been more interested in what [his lady] said' than 'in how [she] spoke' as Davies a 'real lover' was (*AS* 54).

It is a complex image of Davies as a lover and storyteller that emerges from *The True Traveller* (Duckworth, March 1912). The book has a brilliant opening, seeming to plunge the reader into the middle of a conversation with an intriguing, cultivated interlocutor: 'I don't know what it is that has always attracted me to ill-dressed people and squalid places' (*TT* 1). And the reader, artfully assumed to be as broad-minded and tolerant of the ways of the world as the narrator, is kept involved in the performance of storytelling with such remarks as, 'I must confess that, at that time, ... I did not know life as I know it now'; and promises such as 'I will let you know in a future chapter how much the poor, broken, homeless man in London is beholden to this kind of woman' (*TT* 22). Davies's skills as a prose writer are more developed than in the *Autobiography* largely because he is able to project in this book a more frank and confiding voice. The sexual censorship that the *Autobiography* was subject to is lifted here, but more importantly Davies is able to imagine his readers as being as uncensorious as himself. He is able to write about the particulars of things that happened to him as a tramp that makes them seem authentic and even occasionally heartfelt. The success of the book as a whole is Davies's ability to keep turning the stream of observations and anecdotes from one subject or feeling to another – comic, surprising, sentimental, thought-provoking, shocking – and all the time holding our attention.

Davies's sense of being one of life's outsiders makes him deeply sympathetic to prostitutes who also live on the social margins, although he recognises their liveliness as much as their pathos. They are 'courtesans' whose trade is plied in 'a sporting house' in the best of which, like one in Chicago, 'a score of beautiful women were willing to sell their love to any strange man that had enough money' (*TT* 36). Davies hears about this place when he meets a woman in a wood who first makes love to him, then tells him her life story of having to leave her violent husband and make her living in this sporting house. Elements of romance shape this encounter, as the virtuous hero is seduced by the 'strange companion' met in the wood:

> I sat down at her side, with the intention of letting her have her own way, and to take no liberty of my own accord. However, there was no necessity for me to make the least advance, for I was no sooner within her reach than her arms were around me, and I was kissed and hugged until I could not help returning her passion. 'I am not particular about gathering sticks to-day,' she said at last; 'tomorrow will do for that.' (*TT* 37)

This encounter, one of the first told in the book, is one of the most compelling, for the woman goes on to tell him the story of her life.

As in romance it is the woman's story that is more moving than her lovemaking. These fleeting intimacies leave the storyteller deeply affected, feeling how extraordinary it was 'to meet a woman of that kind in the woods', and reflecting, 'I often think of it now' (*TT* 39). Not all Davies's stories are so romantic, though they are nearly all sympathetic to the prostitutes' points of view. He describes women coming from Whitechapel and gathering for business on Westminster Bridge as darkness begins to fall:

> As soon as it became dark I could see that the courtesans were not only increasing in number, but were also becoming bolder, and I knew that their hour had come. In less than ten minutes, when I stood on a street corner, I had been passed and spoken to by several. At last one came boldly up to me and asked if I would go home with her for a short time. (*TT* 260)

As it happens he refuses because he 'did not like the look of her much', but this leads to an analysis of the financial and social exploitation suffered by prostitutes at the hands of their pimps and landladies. In the area of contemporary sexual mores, in which he was expert, Davies was a valuable observer.

There are other remarkable social insights, such as that 'gentlemen' will avoid fighting and would rather be blackmailed, 'however much courage they may have', because to receive marks in a fight is 'a disgrace, whatever account is given of them' (*TT* 124). Fighting is a theme discussed more openly in this book than in the *Autobiography*, along with its corollary, fear. A man going with a prostitute is fearful that he will be attacked and robbed by her pimp; and a prostitute is in constant danger of attack by her clients, though Davies relishes the reversing of this situation by Poll Sanders who learnt from her boxer husband how to fight with her fists. As in his poetry Davies is strongly drawn to women not just for their sexuality but also for their strength and defiance of their usual subordination. He overcomes his hostility to African Americans when he remembers with satisfaction how a young black woman 'with her two hands in her sleeves, had a razor held ready to cut off the ear or nose of any man that provoked her' (*TT* 174). In fact, Davies enjoys seeing weapons skillfully handled and courageously deployed: 'Knowing these things [like the women carrying razors], the reader can imagine my delight when I saw that Yank knew how to use the razor as a weapon' (*TT* 174). And, in the only instance in his writing, he recounts his own violence when he attacked a man for refusing to pay a prostitute. He tells the story with fine, self-deprecating comic skill, for caught as he is between the woman's loud protests and the man's sullenness, he presents himself as being neither gallant nor heroic, thinking he might 'give the woman a shilling out of [his] own pocket, and persuade her to trouble about him no more'. The reluctant hero decides to 'risk the consequences of one attempt' and 'so with one bound I sprang forward and with my open hand pushed his head back with all my force. There was a dull thud and then a groan, and the next moment the man fell to the hard pavement, where he lay without making a move' (*TT* 97). The woman instantly takes money from the man's pocket and disappears.

Stonesifer thought that Davies sentimentalized prostitutes in *The True Traveller*, and certainly Davies is keen to moralise stories of these women giving food to the destitute, which he calls 'their extra-ordinary sympathy for the poor' (*TT* 93). But some affecting moments in the book are more than merely sentimental for they touch on some of Davies's most deeply-felt preoccupations. One such moment occurs when a young woman takes pity on him and looks after him when he is ill. It is only after she has asked him if he will let her be his friend and look after him, and he feels, in accept-ing this offer, like 'falling across the floor at her feet, and making her responsible for whatever happened after' (*TT* 53), that he realises that he is in a 'sporting house' and his nurse is a 'courtesan'. Powerful feelings and fantasies are aroused in him by the woman and the situation. When he leaves he sees 'she was affected at our parting', and he cannot speak 'for fear of breaking down, so affected was I at receiving so much kindness from people of that kind' (*TT* 58). Davies tells the story as being about discovering love in the midst of social and sexual degradation, and emotional and physical vulnerability (of both the young courtesan and the sick beggar). The young woman seems to him to be 'a pure-minded woman with a heart full of kindness'. And he, if only he had the power that 'a fortune' would give him, would offer her 'a pure married life' and a 'home'. Old memories are stirred in him as he takes his leave, for that 'seemed like leaving home and my mother' (*TT* 59, 62). Curiously, the fantasy of recognising the goodness in a courtesan and giving her a better life through marriage anticipated precisely what Davies would turn into reality when he met the young woman who would become his wife. While Davies's respect for and attentiveness to women may be unusual for his or any other time, his suspicion of women's inability to respect books is more conventional. 'Very few women have any reverence for a book', he writes, for they 'bang a book about without thinking that it contains a human mind' (*TT* 197). He is all the more amazed therefore when he enters a young prostitute's room and discovers all around books that she enjoyed buying and reading. The reader is once more fascinated by the storyteller's deft self-presentation of his mixed feelings when he discovers that the woman has read some of his poetry. In a typically comic, self-depreciating way he reacts with pleasure and vanity, and wonders if he should reveal himself as the author. He decides against this, and instead gives her enough money to allow her 'two or three days, without being driven by poverty to seek another strange man' (*TT* 290-1).

While *The True Traveller* lacks the unifying plot lines that both the *Autobiography* and *Young Emma* have, and seems to consist, like the weaker of Davies's prose self-writings, of a string of anecdotes, there is in fact a unifying theme in the notion of freedom. One of the first stories signifies this, as Davies writes how he gave up a job and 'determined ... never to work for a master again' when the master forbade him from laughing while at work (*TT* 15). The demands of regular labour are rejected just as determinedly as the demands of marriage. The book implies that the true traveller is not simply one who begs for a living, but one who lives a sexually free and unencumbered life. And this broader image of freedom does not exclude women too from being true travellers. Freedom is manifested in the book as much in the way its stories are told as in what the are about. Davies's narrator voice is free from the common prejudices and preconceptions about sexual life, and expresses his freedom in finely-turned, often ironical and singular stories. Edward Thomas's asking his poet friends about the relation between their love poems and 'the circumstances under which each was written' was a sign of a cultural change in England around 1910, the first stirrings of modernity. In plays and fiction there was an engagement with controversial social and personal issues in increasingly realistic modes of writing. As Robert H. Ross observes in his insightful study of Georgianism, Archer, Pinero, Jones and Shaw had made 'a successful assault upon the moribund stage' (*GR* 31) and Galsworthy and Bennett had done something similar for fiction. But poetry lagged behind, largely because the poetic innovations of the 1890s were impossible to pursue after the social and artistic catastrophe of the Wilde trials. By the second decade of the twentieth century a way forward for English poets was appearing. Writers' experience was coming to be prized as the basis for good writing, and greater realism as the mode that could represent it. In place of high-flown Victorian rhetoric and attitudinising, and '*fin de siècle* enervation' (*GR* 141), poets came to value immediate experience expressed in fairly simple diction, and aimed at a wide readership. The desire for change, for a modern spirit to find expression, resulted in the publication in December 1912 of *Georgian Poetry 1911-1912*, in which Davies had a significant role. In the words of Robert H. Ross the 'modern poet's task ... at the turn of the decade, was before all else to achieve truth to life' (*GR* 45). 'Georgian' was a brilliant label invented by the enterprising instigator of all the volumes of poetry that were published between 1912 and 1922, Edward Marsh, civil servant and literary middleman; and in it he captured the mood for change. D.H. Lawrence certainly registered its impact and cultural significance when he called the first Georgian collection 'a big breath taken when we were waking up after a night of repressive dreams' (*NP* 87). Rupert Brooke declared that the volume was meant 'to strike a blow for young and eager poets', so it was ironic that Davies, who came to be seen as emblematic of Georgian poetry, was forty-three when it was published.

Davies was in many ways the ideal poet to fit the Georgian archetype. He was politically liberal, with a keen sense of social injustice from direct experience; he was a living exemplar of the potential for cultural improvement of the lower classes; he was manly and loved the outdoors, with no hint of the effeteness of the upper-class poet.

He wrote in simple language and poetic forms, of experiences that were close to him; and could write of natural and physical beauty in authentic ways. If Edward Thomas was the first lucky break of Davies's career then the volumes of *Georgian Poetry* were the second. His poems appeared in each of the five volumes that were published between 1912 and 1922, and the huge sales of the first volumes guaranteed that he became a household name among the people interested in poetry. By the time of the last volume he had an established poetic reputation, but by then the vein of Georgianism was exhausted and more powerful kinds of modernism had overwhelmed this first tentative step towards a new form of writing.

But in September 1911 when the idea of a volume of poetry by some new poets whose work was not yet recognised was decided upon by Edward Marsh and his poet friends, Rupert Brooke, W.W. Gibson, and John Drinkwater, and the editor of *Poetry Review* Harold Munro, there was no conscious intent to start a new poetic movement. The goal was rather to 'foster and develop the newly awakening interest in poetry that seemed to be in the air' (*WHDB* 97). Davies's name was among the first to be mentioned. When Marsh wrote to him he gladly agreed to contribute but wanted to agree with Marsh which of his poems would be chosen. He worked on the poems he wanted included to ensure that they showed him at his most accomplished and polished. With later Georgian volumes he came to trust Marsh enough to let him cut lines from his poems. The poems Davies chose were 'The Kingfisher' from *Farewell to Poesy* (1910) and 'The Child and the Mariner', 'Days Too Short', 'In May', and 'The Heap of Rags' all from *Songs of Joy* (1911).

The critic who wrote in the *Daily News* in January 1913 was surely right that the poets in *Georgian Poetry 1911-1912* all shared 'an intense interest in external things, an intense feeling for their reality and importance' (*GP* 64). Davies's selection demonstrated his pity for the destitute down-and-out sleeping by the Thames in 'The Heap of Rags', but left the political implications unspoken. The poem ends in a stream of metaphorical speculation in which 'nature' is an alternative realm of freedom and beauty to ugly suffering:

> Was it a man that had
> Suffered till he went mad?

So many showers and not
One rainbow in the lot;
Too many bitter fears
To make a pearl from tears. (*SJ* 72)

'The Child and the Mariner' has a ballad's hardboiled impersonality. The other three poems present an idealised natural world of order, sensuousness, and, above all, apparent accessibility to the ordinary person. Davies specifically asked for 'The Kingfisher' to be included in the selection, telling Marsh that it was 'a better poem than any you name' (*GR* 122), and he certainly seems to have sensed what the reading public would like, for that poem has been identified ever since as demonstrating the literary value of the 'lyric gift' so prized by contemporaries and now relatively meaningless at a time when poetry, to be noticed at all, has to perform in many more voices. One critic has called 'The Kingfisher' one of 'the purest lyrics... in the language' (*GP* 378), and what this seems to mean is that the poem represents an authentic outpouring of feeling in response to something in the countryside. The idea is anti-intellectual because it values feeling far above ideas, and it ignores the craft involved in writing. More recently another critic has called the poem phony, and suggested that Davies may have written it to satisfy the desire for the obviously 'poetic' (*PW* 49).

With characteristic insight Edward Thomas identified in Georgian poetry a yearning for simplicity and authenticity in its 'modern love of the simple and primitive, as seen in children, peasants, savages, early men, animals, and Nature in general' (*GP* 67). W.H. Davies fitted into this myth perfectly, and contemporary reviewers were quick to characterise him as just such a primitive and innocent. In supremely patronising comments Walter de la Mare, writing in the *Edinburgh Review* in 1913, called Davies's work 'naif and fresh', adding that his art 'seems to be (yet how can it be?) the purest intuition', for 'Davies loves instinctively all simple things', and 'gives us back the eager absorbed eyes of childhood' (*GP* 112). Davies was in a sense very lucky to have been writing at the moment of the Georgians because he fitted their requirements so well. Had he been writing twenty years earlier or later he would not have appeared significant; but in 1911 his kind of writing suited the fashion. Once again, Edward

Thomas saw clearly how Davies's career had come into fortunate conjunction with contemporary trends; in another review of *Georgian Poetry 1911-1912* he called Davies 'a fortunate accident that might have happened at any time, but did not' (*GP* 91).

Georgian Poetry 1911-1912 was a considerable commercial success, eventually selling fifteen thousand copies and providing its contributors with a handsome return. Davies was delighted of course, writing to Marsh that he 'had performed a wonder, made poetry pay' (*GR* 129). His appearance in all five volumes of Georgian poetry gave him financial security. But he also gained a reputation as a Georgian and so his reputation eventually sank with the reputation of the Georgians as a whole.

This was the second time in his life that Davies had been labelled: first as a tramp poet and second as a Georgian. On balance, he was probably fortunate in appearing to the reading public in these guises for without them he might have remained invisible. But they did define him too narrowly, stereotype him, and prevent readers from seeing the anger of his writing and its skillfullness.

Davies's appearance in the first Georgian anthology propelled him rapidly into London literary society. The Poetry Bookshop, run by Harold Munro, opened in January 1913, and Davies was there meeting Edward Marsh for the first time and obviously taking to him, for eleven days later he entertained Marsh and Rupert Brooke to tea in Sevenoaks. Davies was able to travel to London more often now that he was better off, and there he continued to meet literary friends at the St George and the Mont Blanc restaurants. D.H. Lawrence crossed his path and a brief, awkward friendship began then guttered out at the end of 1913. Lawrence had also appeared in the first Georgian volume, and he and Davies shared similar working-class childhoods, as well as the impulse to write about nature. But while Lawrence regarded nature as a 'part of one's consciousness, virtually a part of one's body' (*WHDB* 102), Davies responded to nature as something separate from the human, as a prompter of finer human feelings. Davies's biographer recounts how Davies had asked Marsh to obtain Lawrence's autograph for him. Lawrence asked if Marsh would arrange a meeting with himself, Frieda, Davies and Marsh himself, and this duly took place in London in July 1913. Lawrence was apparently taken with the Welshman who appeared to be 'the natural man with whom he preoccupied himself' (*WHDB* 103}. Davies was then sent an invitation to join the couple in Germany, and replied that he would visit them when they reached Italy, but this never happened. Davies had meanwhile written to Lawrence that his poetic inspiration was flagging. Unfortunately when Lawrence read Davies's next book of poetry, *Foliage*, he confirmed for himself Davies's fears. In October 1913 he wrote to Marsh with a scathing response to the book, and an analysis of how he thought Davies had lost his creative way. It is worth quoting at length because it was to prove prophetic of Davies's literary decline.

> Poor Davies – he makes me so furious, and so sorry. He's really like a linnet that's got a wee little sweet song, but it only sings when it's wild. And he's made himself a tame bird – poor little devil. He makes me furious ... I think one ought to be downright cruel to him, and drive him back; say to him, Davies, our work is getting like Birmingham tin-ware; Davies, you drop your h's, and everybody is tempering the wind to you, because you are a shorn lamb; Davies, your accent is intolerable in a carpeted room; Davies, you hang on like the mud on a lady's silk petticoat. Then he might leave his Sevenoaks room, where he is rigged up as a rural poet, proud of his gilt mirror and his romantic past: and he might grow his wings again, and chirrup a little sadder song. (*WHDB* 103-4)

Lawrence's short enthusiasm for Davies never reappeared and the brief friendship faded away. Davies apparently remained baffled by Lawrence. *Foliage* was published by Elkin Matthews in September 1913. By now Davies's range of subjects and points of view were familiar to readers, and there's a smoothness in the writing that suggests a comfortable distance from the subjects treated. Walter de la Mare, in a review in the *Times Literary Supplement*, slyly hinted at Davies's limitations: his inspiration was 'not quite so spontaneous as ever', though his art was 'simply second nature' with no 'needless lumber of the intellect'. It is true that the volume consists of what by 1913 had become formulaic Davies, but that formula was less childlike than de la Mare implied. Ezra Pound singled out from

Foliage 'Dreams of the Sea' for the underplayed artfulness of 'its sound quality' nearer to the Elizabethans than to the nineteenth-century poets, as demonstrated particularly by this stanza:

> And I have seen the gentle breeze as soft
>   As summer's, when it makes the cornfields run;
> And I have seen thy rude and lusty gale
>   Make ships show half their bellies to the sun.

The 'curious traditional dialect' that Pound heard here sprang from what he called 'the fine phrase and the still finer simplicity'. Pound clearly recognised in Davies's artistry the achievement of at least one Georgian aim, to write in simple diction. But perhaps de la Mare was also right in admonishing Davies for the repetitiveness of his subjects.

Poetic inspiration was indeed flagging for Davies in 1913, though it is perhaps unsurprising given the prolific period he had just enjoyed. With *The True Traveller* Davies had at last come to the end of the prose accounts of his years as a tramp and beggar in the USA and England. It was therefore only his poetry that he had now to depend on for his continuing reputation as a writer. In 1913, however, he came to feel increasingly unhappy at living in Sevenoaks, and increasingly drawn to London and his growing circle of friends and contacts. The discomforts of the town included having to deal with the demands of the local children whom he had befriended and to whom he gave money and sweets. He may also have had an unsuccessful love affair there in 1913. On top of that his landlady complained about damage to Davies's room. In a letter to Rupert Brooke, Marsh wrote that Davies had left Sevenoaks 'because of the uncertainty of his social position' (*WHDB* 106). It was time to move on, and Davies moved to London in January 1914.

He moved restlessly three times until settling in two rooms at 14 Great Russell Street in 1916 where he stayed until 1922. At a stroke Davies was cut off from the English countryside that had made such a strong, direct impact on his writing, at least in his early years in Kent. But Davies had never been simply a nature poet, though that would increasingly come to be how he was seen both by others and himself. His London life allowed him to become much more of a literary man, maintaining contact with old friends and making new friends, and enjoying his reputation as a poet and man of letters. It was during his London years, between 1914 and 1922, when Davies was to be found mixing with writers, visual artists, and, during the war years, members of high society, and that stories about him and his eccentric behaviour were recorded, usually quite fondly.

Davies's early volumes of poetry written before 1914 exhibited a range of modes and forms and feelings. Increasingly, however, after the publication of the 1912 volume of Georgian poetry he came to be associated with nature poetry and the particular kind of nature writing that was especially highly prized in the early years of the century, the nature lyric. De la Mare's is a typical critical response from the cultural establishment to Davies's poetry, typecasting it as the artless response of a simple soul to the mysterious beauty of nature: 'With a tender, instinctively wise heart he tells his truth ... [that] shames his reader, who never in all his born days ... saw anything quite so sharply and only its beautiful self' (*PV* 134). Although this judgement diminishes the range of Davies's writing, it became the orthodox view of Davies and one that he himself came to accept. It was 'pure lyricism', in Davies's view, that was 'poetry's great height' (*WHDB* 112). Not every fellow writer was struck by Davies's poetic gifts, however. Robert Frost, who had become a friend of Edward Thomas's from their first meeting in 1913, gave Davies a hostile response when he was visited by him in May 1914. The sharp-tongued Frost, who referred to Davies as 'the unsophisticated nature poet of the day – absolutely uncritical untechnical untheoretical', described the encounter, which seems to have brought out the worst in both men, with a nasty sense of superiority:

> We have had a good deal of him at the house for the last week and the things he has said for us to remember him by! He entirely disgusted the Gibsons with whom he was visiting. His is the kind of egotism another man's egotism can't put up with. He was going from here to be with Conrad. He said that would be pleasant because Conrad knew his work *thoroughly*. After waiting long enough to obscure the point we asked him if he knew Conrad's work *thoroughly*. Oh no – was it good? We told him yes. He was glad we liked it. (*FLL* 81)

Lyric poetry depends upon the feelings of the poet for its sub-stance, and the quality of the poetry depends upon how interesting or authentic those feelings are, and how skillfully they can be projected into poetic forms. Davies was certainly conscious of the possibility that his poetry might dry up; as early as 1910 he thought he was writing his *Farewell to Poesy*, and during 1913 he was confiding to D.H. Lawrence that his inspiration was fading. He refused to take a regular job because he feared that that would destroy the feelings that were the source of his poetry. His personality was his most precious resource, and he defended it tenaciously. But critics like de la Mare misrepresented Davies when they described him as being childlike, natural and serene. His feelings were far from serene. More than any-thing he defended his own freedom and independence, but in his isolation strong and conflicting feelings raged. Edward Thomas's daughter, Myfanwy, remembered Davies being so suspicious of other people that he would refuse even to tell tradesmen when he would be at home or away from his cottage. Other friends testified to his sensi-tivities and fears. The painter Laura Knight recalled a visit she made to Great Russell Street. As she went up the stairs to Davies's flat she called out to him, but when she entered he room she found Davies behind the door holding his wooden leg aloft about to strike what he thought was an approaching burglar (*ST* 42). He also feared emo-tional dependence on another person, as several poems testify; in 'A Vagrant's Life' he wrote, 'I fear to give one thing my heart, / That Death or Absence may us part' (*NatP* 51). Many of these fears have been attributed to the years Davies spent on the road or living in doss-houses, when mutual suspicion was endemic and self-defence essential. But after he had become a writer, such behaviour served the deeper purpose of defending the self that served the poetry. Edmund Gosse sensed the emotional conflicts that lay behind Davies's poetry when he reviewed *Georgian Poetry 1911-1912* in January 1913 and identified 'a sense of the torment of existence in Mr. W.H. Davies' (*GP* 75). The war that broke out in November 1914 accentuated that torment.

Five: London Life Among Writers, Artists and High Society 1914-1923

The Bird of Paradise was published on 5 November 1914, and the title poem of the volume, a ballad spoken by a prostitute about her friend dying of venereal disease, invites its readers to take an unmoralised view of her:

> 'Nell Barnes was bad on all you men,
>   Unclean, a thief as well;
> Yet all my life I have not found
>   A better friend than Nell'. (*BP* 85)

When this poem was published in *Georgian Poetry 1913-1915*, the second Georgian collection, one critic called it a piece of 'sheer ugliness', but this view misunderstands Davies's fidelity to his impressions of the world around him, even if it flew in the face of conventional morality. 'The Bird of Paradise' and 'Nell Barnes' are sympathetic to the women they represent, and reflect Davies's determination in the years before and during the war to write about things as he saw them. The public recognition he had achieved strengthened his self-confidence as a respected writer and an interesting man. The respect he received from the ever larger circle of writers and artists whom he got to know, also boosted his self-esteem, and, just as significantly, exposed him to new artistic influences. At a time when the subjects that could be treated by writers were limited by narrow codes of propriety, and when Rupert Brooke was scornfully denouncing poets who thought, as he said, that literary realism 'is a fearless reproduction of what real living men say when there is a clergyman in the room', Davies was writing and publishing some truly realist poems.

The two ballads are the most original poems in *The Bird of*

Paradise, and prefigure the best of Davies's poems which were to emerge from the stresses of the war years in *Forty New Poems* in 1918. But other poems essay technical innovations in verse form, feeling, or voice. A poem about children trying to wake their dead mother uses 6-stress, 12-syllable lines and childlike diction to achieve its touching, sentimental effect:

> They press the pillow on their mother's face and head;
> They take her by the arm to pull her out of bed –
> And still that mother sleeps and will not wake and play. (*BP* 46)

'The Child Chatters' is written as a nursery rhyme in the voice of a child addressing God, though with a twist of adult humour as the child thinks about the devil challenging God:

> And if he bothers you too much
>   And you're afraid, and you sleep bad,
> Then, God which art in Heaven, you must
>   Have whisky, like my Dad. (*BP* 69)

Humour in all of Davies's writing is often rather simple.

Poems in *The Bird of Paradise* pay attention to the erotic attractions of women, but also to the suffering in women's lives, as in 'The Collier's Wife':

> Oh, collier, collier, underground,
>   In fear of fire and gas,
>   What life more danger has?
> Who fears more danger in this life?
> There is but one – thy wife! (*BP* 75)

But along with this sensitivity to others goes the poet's sense of life passing and death. In 'Plants and Men' it is

> Sweet buds, fair flowers,
> Hard berries then –
> Such is the life
> Of plants and men (*BP* 39).

The poet projects one version of himself as 'The Wanderer' in a chilling fantasy of self-sufficiency, wandering through the countryside,

His best friends fancies of the mind;
More faithful friends by far then he
Shall find in human company.

The wanderer

Lives his simple life,
And has not risked it with a wife (*BP* 53).

Freedom is more precious even than the consolations of a partner, but in 'Her Absence' the poet thinks how having a loving wife might redeem his ageing self and past time by absorbing their memories and then returning them multiplied, an idea represented in the unromantic metaphor of interest on capital:

So do these precious moments glide
    Into her being, where they store;
Until I clasp her as my bride,
    And get them back with thousands more;
Where they have banked in her sweet breast,
And saved themselves with interest. (*BP* 51)

The poet was forty-three years old in 1914 and, after his move from Sevenoaks to London, he seems to have been reflecting on his life, and particularly his single state – assuming that his poems truly indicate his states of mind. Since Davies was an intelligent man, he was always capable of achieving a remarkable detachment from others and indeed himself. In the *Autobiography* and the other tramp books he writes about his fellow beggars from his own point of view, and in many poems he observes and analyses as often as he simply celebrates. His abiding desire for personal freedom expressed itself in his tramping and in avoiding a regular job; but just as importantly in his determination to form his own responses to things, to trust those responses, and protect them as a source of his writing's value and originality. If tramping is the body's liberty then this is the mind's; and a poem of that name in *The Bird of Paradise* demonstrates how it works. In 'The Mind's Liberty' he is walking through London and is reminded by the dome of St Paul's of a Welsh hill. This commonplace idea is transformed, however, by Davies's introducing his strongly eroticised imagination into the poem – perhaps this was one of the times when he was trying to make a pick-up. The resulting metaphor fuses dome, hill and woman's breast into one complex response:

> And when I'm passing near St Paul's,
>> I see, beyond the dome and crowd,
> Twm Barlum, that green pap in Gwent,
>> With its dark nipple in a cloud. (*BP* 23)

The mind's liberty lies not just in thinking about Gwent while walking in the London streets but in being able to experience the world through intimate inward desires.

Davies's return to London marked a turning point from relative solitude and introversion to sociability, and to developing an identity as an established writer. It was much easier for him to meet old literary friends at their gatherings at the Mont Blanc restaurant, Soho, and the St George's restaurant in St Martin's Lane. And when he went to the Poetry Bookshop's opening in January 1913 he extended his range of literary acquaintance to include Henry Newbolt, F.S. Flint, Robert Frost, and Edward Marsh. Once he was living in London Davies was able to meet George Bernard Shaw for the first time, as well as Alice Meynell, Conrad Aiken, and John Freeman. From now on he was to be a notable figure on the literary scene.

He also became well known on the artistic scene, in demand to sit for artists, and often forming friendships with them. He met the New Yorker Jacob Epstein in the early years of the war when Epstein was renting an attic room above Harold Munro's Poetry Bookshop and using a nearby garage as his studio. Epstein's portrait sculptures at this time were often of heads which suggested the sitter's sympathetic personality in striking physical forms. Certainly he and Davies got on well. Davies's awareness that Epstein was a man sensitive to real or imagined slights helped them get along: 'he was not suspicious of me', Davies wrote in *Later Days* (177). The American Jew and the working-class Welshman who were both aspiring to become artists had no doubt experienced social prejudice. Epstein asked Davies to sit for him the first time they met, and Davies agreed provided he received in exchange a cast of the bronze sculpture for himself. Davies paid ten pounds, the cost of the bronze for his copy. Of the six bronzes cast, one went to the Hon. Evan Morgan, later Viscount Tredegar, who later donated it to Newport Museum and Art Gallery where it can still be seen. Epstein's portrait has been judged to be one of the finest portraits of Davies because it catches the handsomeness and strength of his head along with his alertness and sensitivity. Epstein aimed at 'an empathetic reading of personality or mood' in his portrait sculptures (*SE* 34), and to achieve this he would happily produce unflattering, distorted forms. But with the sculpture of Davies there is no distortion, which suggests that Davies's personality was to be found in the natural form of his face, and that Epstein was sympathetic to that personality. In Epstein Davies was meeting an artist who, unlike himself, was in the artistic avant garde, but with some shared artistic interests. One aspect of Epstein's modernity was his determination to find ways to sculpt human sexuality 'as unselfconsciously as anything else' (*SE* 28), an ambition that Davies would have responded to since he had been unobtrusively realising it himself. Epstein's work possessed what one critic has called a 'virile intensity' that Davies's work also sometimes has.

The Epstein bust set off in Davies a new passion to own works of art. 'I was suddenly seized', he wrote 'with an avaricious spirit to possess beautiful works of art, and wanted a John, a Sickert and others to go with it' (*LD* 160). He had a chance to own a Sickert, for Walter Sickert and other artists in the Camden Town Group lived close to Davies's flat in Great Russell Street in the area known as Fitzrovia. Sickert was inspired by 'The Bird of Paradise' to paint a picture based on it, 'The Blackbird of Paradise' showing a young woman with prominent teeth and beaky features giving a broad smile in response to something or someone outside the canvas. She appears animated and frank, and her black clothes and hat with feathers come from the title of Davies's poem. More significantly both artist and poet represent realistically and sympathetically an undecorous, independent woman. Sickert was a leading member of the group of artists that established themselves in 1911 as the Camden Town Group, specialising in depicting scenes from everyday life in a mildly post-impressionist manner. They were the painterly equivalent of the Georgian poets, though they responded to the city more than the country, and were a moderate English man-ifestation of the modernist impulses emanating from continental Europe. Harold Gilman and William Rothenstein were members of Sickert's group, and both become friends of Davies. However, Davies's reaction to some of these artists' modernist techniques indicates the limits of his own modernity. Gilman, who was noted for his portraits containing bands of strong, non-realistic colour, offered to paint Davies's portrait; but Davies refused, saying that Gilman

> was then in an experimental stage and had strange ideas of colour .... I did not want Gilman to paint my face blotched and purple, like the face of a drowned man who has been found after many days in the water (*PW* 74-75).

The joke captures something of Gilman's style, but it also shows Davies's *amour propre* when it came to the image he wanted to project now that he had become a prominent poet. Certainly Sickert valued Davies's judgement in matters of visual art for he told Osbert Sitwell, who dutifully recorded it in his memoirs, that no one understood his painting and then along came this old tramp and instinctively understood everything. Sickert made a number of drawings of Davies in preparation for an etching of him. Seizing the moment, Davies offered Sickert an example of his writing in exchange for one of Sickert's works. Sickert accepted and Davies chose from the six paintings then in his studio the small oil painting of 'Wellington House Academy' which Sickert then inscribed to him. Davies's recognition by distinguished artists as a man with a fine critical eye boosted his self-confidence. He was able to see himself as a respected fellow artist in a parallel but separate area, and, although the artists' world had its own snobberies and jealousies, they were not those of writers, to which Davies was specially sensitive.

Davies had great fun meeting artists. He may have met Sickert at the first artists' party he went to in Frith Street, Soho (though the details of Davies's memoirs in *Later Days* are no more to be trusted than those in *The Autobiography of a Super-Tramp*). In 1917 Davies met the artist Nina Hammet at a party given by the Sitwells, and she took him up 'as one of her special pets', as Stonesifer puts it. He was sitting on the floor and she approached him in her golden evening dress with a wreath of autumn leaves round her head 'like a dissipated Bacchante after a little champagne', sat on the floor next to him, and 'talked of the relative values of beer and public houses', as she recalls in her splendidly entitled memoirs, *Laughing Torso*. Hammet became one of the growing list of painters who persuaded Davies to sit for them, though he probably didn't require much persuasion; but her painting showed Davies with a bottle and glass in the foreground, which displeased him, and he told her it made him look like a 'gaunt sick wreck of a drunkard, who was in the act of drinking himself to death'. Davies was sensitive on the subject of drink since he had had periods of self-destructive drunkenness in the past, and had become over-sensitive about his reputation.

Opinion about Davies among London writers and artists was mixed and changing. One factor to be taken into account was his estimate of himself, which had at its core an irreducible sense of his artistic power and value, but which was also affected by others' judgements of him. As his standing grew and was consolidated in the second decade of the century, so his sense of his own importance as a poet quite properly increased too. But some of the praise heaped on him as a phenomenon, a primitive with a prodigious talent, tempted him into a false sense of himself. As the years went by it was this narrow image of Davies that came to dominate the public mind, and that he himself increasingly succumbed to. In 1926 the critic F.L. Lucas wrote about this distorting view of the poet, and its deleterious effects on his poetry, saying the trouble was that

> though other modern poets have more admirers, none have more adorers than Mr. Davies. They have erected their concep-tion of him into a sort of idyllic idol, an inspired natural, a poetic Peter Pan of bucolic complexion, contemplating, with poesy and a straw in his mouth, the loves of the butterflies ... Isn't he too delightfully naive? – Oh, Mr. Davies, do be naive again! And in a few months Mr. Davies is naive again. The thing comes to seem, if it does not actually become, a trick. (*WHDB* 122)

Here, the poet's adorers who harm him speak in an upper-class manner, and certainly, as he moved during the war years more and more into upper-class artistic and social circles, Davies was sub-jected to much of this thoughtless flattery. He resisted most of it, but some inevitably sank in and deceived him.

At least one critic of *Georgian Poetry 1913-1915*, published in 1915, in which Davies had nine poems, suspected him of being deliberately 'simpler ... than anyone has a right to be nowadays' (*GP* 128). That 'nowadays' was particularly telling in the midst of a war, when the ways that writers should respond to an extraordinary situation were coming into question. The conservative critic Arthur Waugh longed for 'the true spirit of beauty which fills Mr Davies's pastoral poems' and railed against the ugliness of 'The Bird of Paradise' which seemed to him to be a sign of larger, more dangerous political changes in society, namely 'the defiance, and consequent loss, of authority which attend all efforts to democratise society and art' (*GP* 156). At the same time Davies was also being buffeted by criticism that saw his contribution to this collection as being as

> charming and naively simple as he used to be, but [with] nothing behind it all; it is beautiful but flimsy: it seems almost at times as if he had exhausted his theme (*GP* 166).

If these critics seem to be reacting to different poets, that is because Davies's writing did indeed have several facets and was written in distinct styles. But the comments pointing out disingenuous simplicity and poetic exhaustion were ominous, for they anticipated later negative judgements on the poet's work. The poems chosen for the second Georgian volume came from *Foliage* (1913) and *The Bird of Paradise* (1914), and while several of them are written in Davies's direct, demotic style – 'Thunderstorms', 'The Mind's Liberty', 'The Bird of Paradise' – others are loaded down with redundant poeticisms and thinness of feeling, such as 'The Moon', 'A Great Time', or 'The Hawk'. In Davies's earlier poetry the occasional crudities of verbal technique or banality of feeling could give it a rough-hewn authenticity, and suggest the vigour of a still-developing artist. In these poems however, conventional technical facility and old-fashioned poeticisms tend to expose weakness of inspiration, as in 'The Hawk':

> Thou dost not fly, thou art not perched,
>   The air is all around:
> What is it that can keep thee set,
>   From falling to the ground? (*BP* 44)

The oddly divergent judgements that critics made on the poems in *Georgian Poetry 1913-1915* may well have been a result of Davies's own divergent modes of writing, and they in turn may have resulted from his uncertainty about who his readers were. Poems like 'The Bird of Paradise' and 'Sweet Stay-at-Home' rely on what Jonathan Barker calls plain language and artful simplicity; but others which use high flown clichés to seem poetic simply end up being phoney. The two manners that Barker detects in Davies's poetry – one that 'fits exactly the right words to the thought expressed in economic and concretely modern imagery', and the other that displays its artistry 'to impress the reader' (*PW* 48, 51) – are starkly on display in the 1915 Georgian volume. The weak poetic manner may have been the result of Davies's faltering poetic inspiration in 1913, and of trying too hard to please the literary authorities, real or imagined. After he moved to London and engaged directly with writers and artists, his writing began once again to recover its economy and confidence, and indeed showed the influence of those modern painters and writers whom he met, among whom were men at the forefront of modern artistic developments like Lawrence and Epstein.

As we have seen, Davies's poverty had been alleviated by the annual Civil List pension of fifty pounds granted in 1911 at the instigation of Edward Thomas. In 1914 Davies was able to return Thomas's favour by writing to Edward Garnett asking him to contact the Royal Literary Fund on Thomas's behalf. While Davies was now financially fairly secure, Thomas continued to exist near the edge of ruin, entirely dependent for his income on book commissions and reviewing, and Davies was sensitive to his friend's plight. For Davies, his contribution to *Georgian Poetry 1913-1915* brought him more royalties than he had ever earned from his previous books. Of all the Georgian volumes, the second's total sales of 19,000 was the greatest, 4,000 more than the first, and greater than the third's 16,000, the fourth's 15,000 and the 8,000 of the last. As a contributor to every volume Davies benefited from these vast sales, and was able to say in 1921 that he was 'always in the public eye, because of all these anthologies that are appearing' (*WHDB* 101). Davies's unlikely dream of living off his earnings as a writer (and avoiding a job) was being realised, helped in 1915 by his Civil List pension being increased to a hundred pounds.

As Michael Holroyd puts it in his biography of Augustus John, at its start the war in France was itself seen as the enemy by all artists. To begin with they ignored it, but eventually it affected their lives in one way or another. Davies's powers of detachment preserved him from the initial war hysteria, but in time he too came to feel the pressures of the war albeit in indirect ways. In Wales the outbreak of war was greeted eagerly, and men enlisted in their thousands to a total of 280,000 men by 1918, a higher proportion than either England or Scotland. The Welshman Lloyd George was prime minister, and he encouraged patriotic support for the war among people for whom pacific liberalism had long held sway. At the eisteddfod of 1915 Lloyd George was warmly received when he invoked Wales's long distant military past as a model for the war aim of defending small nations. In 1917 the man who won the bardic chair at that year's eisteddfod, Hedd Wyn of Trawsfynydd, was killed in action, and this set off 'a patriotic display of mourning quite equal to any English outpouring over Rupert Brooke' (*HMW* 343). From this kind of war enthusiasm Davies was immune, and no trace finds its way into his poetry written during these years. Davies was too old for military service, even if his disability had not rendered him unfit for active service. He did however contribute to the war effort by taking part in fund raising readings organised by upper-class women.

The war years were difficult for Davies. In 1914 the cottage properties that had provided an income over the years for him and his brother and sister had fallen into disrepair and were without tenants, and for a year no income was produced. Davies's financial position worsened, but those of his mother, brother and half-sister were even worse, so Davies gave them money from the little he had. For many years he had been providing financial support for members of his family from his own meagre resources. When his sister Matilda had left her husband and gone to Canada with her lover, she also left four children to be looked after. At the start of the war the three boys emerged from the orphanage where their mother's departure had placed them, needing financial help to earn a living. Davies supported them as they learned farming, then subsidised their emigration to Canada. Hollingdrake's researches have shown how

Davies had earlier helped three of his mother's children from her second marriage to emigrate to Canada (*PW* 38). Davies's friends turned once more to the Royal Literary Fund to try to increase his pension, but the new chairman, Sir Edmund Gosse, did not regard Davies with favour and it took Edward Marsh, one of the initiators of the Georgian poetry project, and now the private secretary of the prime minister, Asquith, to put in a good word for Davies to Gosse. Davies got the increase in his pension in December 1915. The weeks of waiting for a decision activated Davies's paranoid fears of being spied upon, in this case by Mrs Asquith, the prime minister's wife. He avoided pubs and prostitutes, and stayed in his rooms for six weeks, to escape the spies he believed had been set to observe him. These absurd fears may have been fed by stories of the real government spies who were pursuing conscientious objectors and political subversives, and by the increasing social tensions of the war.

War shortages meant less paper for books, and so Davies's 1916 volume of poetry, *Child Lovers*, consisted of only 29 pages and 20 poems, compared with the previous book, *The Bird of Paradise*, with its 86 pages and 47 poems. *Child Lovers* benefits from this economy, for it gives a sense of coherence to its short lyrics which are mostly subtle and complex in feeling, and dwell to an unusual extent on life and death, ghosts and graves. Extreme emotions, that might seem distorted or abnormal, are expressed in wholly convincing ways. 'Friends', for example, deploys very simple language, and sparse rhymes to convey strong, elusive feelings:

> They're creeping on the stairs outside,
>   They're whispering soft and low;
> Now up, now down, I hear his friends,
>   And still they come and go.
>
> The sweat that runs my side, from that
>   Hot pit beneath my shoulder,
> Is not so cold as he will be,
>   Before the night's much older.

This is subtle, direct writing that gives a sense of the twists of feeling produced by the situation; but there's a further unexpected twist in the last verse:

And since I'll have so many friends,
    When on my death-bed lying –
I wish my life had more love now,
    And less when I am dying. (*CL* 21)

Davies's contribution to the war effort from early 1916 was to help raise funds by taking part in poetry readings organised by upper-class society women in London. This gave him an *entrée* into another social world from that of artists and painters (though there was some overlap with artists and writers), no less strange and alien than the world of tramps and beggars, and, like that world, one in which he could satisfy his appetite for experience as well as find a place, and earn respect from people very unlike himself. According to Davies's account in *Later Days*, it was in Byron's old house in Piccadilly that the first reading took place, with Yeats and Belloc being there alongside Davies, who found to his delight that he could perform his own verse with great success. When Ezra Pound heard him read at a charity event he wrote to Harriet Monroe telling her how impressed he had been with Davies's reading, and adding the interesting qualification that the poetry would not be convincing in print, and must lose 'a lot by not having them done by his own voice' (*WHDB* 119). Through the charity poetry readings Davies gained entry into London high society, where he was invited to dinners, and to weekends in country-houses, by such distinguished people as the Asquiths, Lady Ritchie (Thackeray's daughter), Lady Cunard, and Lady Randolph Churchill. They loved to encounter a poet with a colourful past, and Davies loved to join the world of the rich and powerful through which he moved 'like an astonished but very shrewd child' (*WHDB* 120). Davies had the chance to exercise his skills of self-dramatisation, and to present himself, with the pre-rogative of the poet, as a man of authentic feeling. Lady Ritchie was delighted to meet a man who had earned a living by manual labour, 'like the common men we meet in the street' (*LD* 136) – just the sort of situation that Evelyn Waugh and E.F. Benson so delighted in in their fiction. At their worst, the upper classes treated Davies as a harmless pet who would amuse and titillate them. And while Davies was indeed a sincere and frank man whose personal qualities were, according to Aldous Huxley, 'most refreshing in a world where there was apt to be affectation and an excessive display of cleverness', he still had what Pound called a 'peasant's shrewdness' and could 'look at the British analytically', seeing 'things that others didn't' (*WHDB* 120). Among the English upper classes Davies deployed the same survival skills he had learnt in the beggar camps of the United States and in the doss-houses of London, adapting to the demands of the subculture, but still observing it keenly and with considerable detachment. What threatened him among the upper classes was not physical violence but condescension, to which he was very sensitive. Occasions when Davies was simply snubbed have not been recorded, but others when Davies suspected an insult when none was intended sometimes have been, usually to suggest his naivety. On one visit to a country house, Davies was embarrassed that his one piece of luggage compared unfavourably with the many pieces of other guests, and expressed this embarrassment to his hostess. When she tried to overcome this awkwardness by suggesting that Davies might like to have a bath after his journey from London, he then suspected another attempt to humiliate him, and told his hostess that he did not need a bath since he had had his bath the previous day (*WHDB* 123). Despite suspected insults or real ones flowing from what a friend of Davies's called the 'arrogant illiteracy' of some members of the upper class, Davies very much enjoyed his forays into this world. The quality of his conversation can be gauged from his own, no doubt polished, accounts in *Later Days*, which are gossipy, ironical, self-mocking, arch and at times slyly suggestive.

By 1916 there were other signs of Davies's growing reputation. He sat for a portrait by William Rothenstein that was to be used later that year as the frontispiece to his *Collected Poems* by the American publisher Alfred A. Knopf. Each of the future editions of the *Collected Poems* had a different portrait of Davies as its frontispiece, testifying to Davies's involvement with artists: the 1923 edition had Augustus John's portrait; that of 1928 used Epstein's bust; and the 1940 edition had the portrait by Laura Knight. Also in 1916 there appeared the first academic study of his poetry in Mary C. Sturgeon's *Studies of Contemporary Poets* published by Harrap. In 1917 one of Jacob Epstein's castings of his bronze bust of Davies was presented to Newport. And the next year Davies was accorded the accolade of an entry in *Who's Who*. The publication in November 1916 of *Collected Poems* in Britain and the United States confirmed his status as an established, respected poet.

As the war ground on, and the death toll mounted with no sign of victory for either side, so fear and insecurity increased among civilians. Davies has left a record of this in *Later Days*, where he recalled how

> while our soldiers were fighting abroad, with shot and shell, the people at home were conducting a civil war among themselves, insulting each other on every occasion they met. Friends quarrelled without reason, and all because of the high strain on their nerves. (p.112)

It was only after the war was over, he added, that he realised 'how terrible were those days; when thousands went mad, and almost everyone reached the point of madness'. Civilians like Davies had to endure passively what the war brought without any power to influence its outcome. They merely awaited news of the men who had gone off to fight. One piece of terrible news came in 1917 when Davies heard that Edward Thomas had been killed in the offensive at Arras. Thomas, his first and most important literary patron and supporter, had come to mean much more to Davies who 'took to Thomas as a brother' (*ETP* 248). They saw each other regularly over the years of their friendship, going for long walks in the country or meeting in London with other literary friends, and Davies often spent Christmas with the Thomas family. Davies found love and security with the Thomas family, talking frankly to Edward and Helen about his sexual life, and seeing at close quarters their passionate feelings for each other. Thomas's biographer believes that the emotional effect on Davies of his friendship with the Thomases was profound, with the trust and security of their friendship preparing the way 'for the quiet happiness that Davies eventually found in his late marriage' (*PW* 64). For Thomas, Davies represented something that he aspired to be, the non-literary man, 'free to think or better still not to think at all, but to let the wind and the rain do my thinking for me, filling my brain' (*ETP* 307). When Thomas himself turned to writing poetry, he showed some of it to close friends, including Davies, without disclosing its authorship. Davies did not recognise the merits of the three poems he was shown, and said they were the work of Robert Frost; a reaction that hurt Thomas, and that Davies regretted. Despite this, Davies was one of the friends who saw Thomas off to the front for the last time in January 1917. He was tired after an all-day sitting with Epstein but was, he later wrote, 'glad to be there'. He and Thomas 'walked up Charing Cross Road together, silently, and neither of us feeling comfortable' (*WHDB* 116). The moving poem that Davies wrote on Thomas's death, 'Killed in Action (Edward Thomas)', remembers the time before the war, the year 1906 when Davies lived at Stidulph's Cottage, when he and Thomas walked the surrounding area:

> And we have known those days, when we
>> Would wait to hear the cuckoo first;
> When you and I, with thoughtful mind,
>> Would help a bird to hide her nest,
> For fear of other hands less kind.

But this action of protecting the vulnerable nest from being despoiled, and the bucolic innocence it recalls, is set against Thomas's death and the fact that there is little consolation to be found in 1917 in the natural world which seems deranged; a once ideal world now turned into an alien, comfortless place of screaming birds and sullen clouds:

> Happy the man whose home is still
>> In Nature's green and peaceful ways;
> To wake and hear the birds so loud,
>> That scream for joy to see the sun
> Is shouldering past a sullen cloud. (*FNP* 22)

The poem expresses with masterful simplicity the poet's personal loss along with the general loss of the war.

Edward Thomas's poems were first published under the pseudonym Edward Eastaway in 1915; and it was not until 1917, after his death, that his *Poems* were published under his own name. In an article Davies noted with some bitterness how poetic fame had come too late for Thomas to enjoy, how in spite of keeping his poems going continually from editor to editor, [Thomas] did not succeed in getting one accepted not even one! How quickly these editors have changed their minds.

(*WHDB* 117)

Davies's own fame was sustained by the publication of the third volume of *Georgian Poetry 1916-1917* in 1917. The public's appetite for poetry was increased by the war, and the Georgian poetry volumes offered a world to escape to from the comfortless reality of wartime Britain. Davies had four poems in this third Georgian collection, all from *Child Lovers* of 1916, and they were judged by one reviewer to be 'just such excellent pieces as he has always written', though he added a sting in the tail that Davies was 'not ashamed to sing the same song a hundred times over' (*GP* 202). All Davies's poems would offer comfort to civilian readers or those in the armed forces in their invocation of scenes of English pastoral peace. 'The White Cascade', described by the *Times Literary Supplement* reviewer as an 'absolutely Daviesian poem' (*GP* 206), probably recalls an American waterfall 'That has a ten-mile voice and shines as far', though it too expresses longing for a lost past:

> Though I may never leave this land again,
> Yet every spring my mind must cross the main
>
> To hear and see that water-bird and star
> That on the mountain sings, and shines so far. (*CL* 14)

Edward Shanks' judgement on Davies's writing in 1926 applies particularly to these poems in the Georgian anthology: that although Davies's experience of nature is

> less rich and less deep [than some other poets] ... all his poetry is one in expressing an innocently sensual appreciation of the delights of the world. (*GP* 331)

Sweet words about the natural world were an antidote to many readers in 1917 to the sufferings brought about by the war. For the writer, they were images of order and calm that were at odds with a personality driven by tumultuous feelings. During the war Davies's fears and obsessions grew. His rooms in Great Russell Street were infested with mice and, Davies feared, rats which he dreaded. To keep them at bay he slept each night with a light on, and placed a saucer of milk-soaked bread at his door. He was afraid of disease, particularly venereal disease, and would have periods of dread that he might have become infected; not an unreasonable fear given his regular use of prostitutes and the limited medications available. He deeply feared the police, a hangover from his days as a tramp. The story he tells in *Later Days* of his encounter with the police shows his paranoia about them. He complained to the police about the noise made by the woman next door, but when a policeman comes round to investigate it, he starts by telling Davies about his own problems with neighbours; and then reveals that he has been ordered by his superiors to keep a watch on Davies himself.

> 'No, no,' I said, hastily, 'you mean number 15, and not 14. My next-door neighbour is number 15, but *I* am number 14.'
> 'There is not the least mistake,' he answered, 'our orders are to keep a sharp eye on number 14.' (*LD* 117-18)

This is sufficiently Kafkaesque to be both funny and disorientating. Certainly Davies's friends laughed when he refused to enter any pubs during the weeks in 1915 when an increase in his civil list pension was being considered by the authorities, convinced as he was that spies had been set on him by Mrs Asquith to discover his 'bad character' and so stop a rise in his pension. He feared the surveillance and judgement of the powerful, reacting with extreme shyness in social situations, and quickly taking offence at a suspected jibe. He relates how he and W.H. Hudson would often be the first to arrive for the lunchtime writers' gatherings at the Mont Blanc restaurant, and how they would sit in awkward silence unable to find any topic for conversation. A nasty misunderstanding occurred at a dinner party given by the artist William Nicholson where Davies met, and took offence at, Max Beerbohm. Beerbohm asked him how long it had been since Shaw had discovered him, a question in which Davies felt there was something wrong, and that 'would be dangerous to answer'. But he said that it was about fifteen years, to which Beerbohm said, 'Oh dear, dear – and has it been going on all this time!' Davies took immediate offence, under-standably, given the ambiguity of Beerbohm's words, taking him to mean that 'it was about time [he] was forgotten'. Beerbohm then apparently tried to retrieve the situation by saying to Davies that Shaw recognised him as 'a real poet' and was trying to help 'a lame dog over the stile'. This phrase deeply wounded Davies since he was, as he wrote in his account of the incident, indeed lame 'and the expression was not figurative, as it would have been with others', and he was left feeling 'dazed and half-stunned' (*LD* 190-91). But Davies was told by his host that his reaction was unwarranted. Beerbohm himself deeply regretted the offence he had caused, and went so far as to write to *The Times Literary Supplement* to explain how he had been misunderstood and how he hoped Davies would write to acknowledge his mistake. But Davies did not budge from his sense of insult, perhaps feeling, quite justifiably, that having been subject to a condescending if not deliberately insulting remark, he was then being asked to subordinate his understanding of the sit-uation to the one asserted by his social and cultural superiors. Davies's adherence to his own point of view, even when it was mis-taken or even paranoid, was the counterweight to what he lacked in class authority. Augustus John recalled how Davies had arrived one day with a sheaf of clippings about himself, the proof of his achieve-ments and identity. And other friends remembered how Davies would refer proudly to his doss-house past to assert his sense of self. Davies's insecurities made him advertise his modest fame and posi-tion in transparent and sometimes comical ways, but he was indeed 'haunted by the fear of losing' what he had achieved; so much so that it produced a persecution complex in him (*WHDB* 110).

The Welshman Augustus John was drawn to Davies's remarkable physiognomy and personality – 'this little man of genius' as he called him in his autobiography – whom he imagined, as he was painting him, to be 'one inspired; his hands clasped before him, his eyes focused, as it were, on Paradise, and his ears, it might be, intent on the song of an invisible bird' (*WHDB* 126). John was the most famous painter of his day, and acted extravagantly the part of the romantic artist. He was drawn to other free, romantic spirits, and used gypsies, tramps and travellers as models, as well as the country people of west

Wales where he spent many summers with an eccentric menage. He was a man in whom, like Davies, 'a passion for personal liberty and entire independence was primary' (*MEP* 1:177). At the Cafe Royal he was a dominating figure among the clientele, exuberantly imagined by Michael Holroyd in his biography of John as

> raucous-voiced sportsmen; alchemists and sorcerers ... a grave contingent from the British Museum; well-dressed gangs of blackmailers, bullies, pimps and *agents–provocateurs* ... intoxicated social reformers and Anglo-Irish jokers ... [and] the exquisite herd of Old Boys from the Nineties. (417)

Among these Davies must have passed unnoticed. John was fascinated by the famous, but particularly famous writers, and he painted several including Ronald Firbank, Oliver St John Gogarty, Arthur Symons, and Bernard Shaw. His oil portrait of Davies is considered by Stonesifer to be best of all the Davies portraits, with its clearly delineated form and the intensity it captures in the eyes of its subject. It is certainly the most romantic of all the portraits of Davies, suggesting the writer to be a sensitive soul, with his full, sculptured lips and dark, liquid eyes looking up towards some distant imagined ideal. Davies's account of sitting for the portrait punctures some of the painting's dreaminess when he writes that he only wanted to sit still, so fixed his eyes on 'a little eye of light that came peeping through a curtain .... But after I had been looking at that small light for about a quarter of an hour, it began to grow and advance into the room' (*LD* 179). Davies came to dislike the portrait that John had made of him, which to unsympathetic eyes might suggest the image of a sensitive horse, and years later referred to the drawing that John made at the same time and presented to him as a 'caricature' by John (*WHDB* 127).

In March 1918 Davies's *A Poet's Pilgrimage* was published, a composite account of several walks that Davies had regularly made, fused into one walk from west Wales eastward. After those years when tramping was a necessity, and begging his means of support, he had regularly set off alone on walking trips with enough money for food, beer, and a bed for the night. He has now become, he writes, 'a literary tramp', not a true traveller. The journey he writes about in the book has been traced by Sybil Hollingdrake in *The Super-Tramp*, who discovered that Davies regularly visited his half-sister Alice and her family in Newport during the war. Certainly Davies writes of Newport with a sense of belonging, as the place where he was 'loved and respected by everyone'. Things are different when he travels west for there he is regarded with suspicion as an English-speaker, and in the small valley towns he is also regarded with suspicion as an outsider. Setting off from Carmarthen he finds himself treated like a stranger worth exploiting when he is overcharged for bread and cheese in an inn, and then cheated by a Swansea landlady. Davies certainly registers the difference between the Welsh-speaking people he meets and himself, referring to 'real Welsh people' with 'their own language' (*PP* 76). Once he reaches Neath he can write that he saw very little there 'to remind me of the Welsh people' (*PP* 74). Davies's sensitivity to the way people react to him make him a valuable sensor of social relations, and he is aware of Welsh speakers' fears of exploitation if they are forced to speak English. Like all Davies's prose memoirs, this is written with detachment, and avoids anything but superficial generalisations. He records his impressions, and his own reactions to what he encounters; and it is his curious personality that makes him notice things from an unusual angle. But his knowledge of Wales leads to some shrewd comments. When he enters the valley towns, where fierce tribal rivalries between adjacent places can lead to fights, he is safe in pubs if he says he is a stranger in town. These are towns where the occupation of the men of the poorer classes are 'singing, football and fighting' (*PP* 107). He is an outsider wherever he goes in Wales, except for Newport and the surrounding area, and he goes tramping armed with 'a stout cane, in which was a strong, sharp toledo blade' (*PP* 130).

He declares himself to be someone dedicated to 'seek beauty and, finding it, give full leisure to its enjoyment' (*PP* 85). And he dislikes signs of industrial life, like railway lines and coal wagons, especially if they impinge on scenes of conventional rural beauty. On the train from Glyn–Neath to Aberdare he sees scenery 'that was sublime', but more often he sees 'wretched dirty little houses [like] so many in Wales' (*PP* 105). Unlike the Futurists who revelled in the machine, or W.H. Auden who found beauty in the industrial landscape between Wolverhampton and Birmingham, Davies finds little to please his romantic aesthetic in industrial south Wales. The one scene that moves him most deeply is near Newport, and it is not merely a landscape, but one that contains memories of himself as a boy. The town's location on the sides of hills makes it 'very beautiful' in Davies's mind, and from Stow Hill it offers impressive sights of the Bristol Channel, 'the islands in it, and the outward and homeward-bound ships':

> But the most beautiful part of Newport is the green country called Alteryn, which has a clear canal coming down lock by lock, with Twm-Barlum in the distance. I had not been in Newport long before I went walking in that direction ... When I was well out of town and stood on a hillside road where I could see down into that wonderful green valley, I became deeply affected at the sight. For there was not the least change; there were the same few little cottages that I had seen so often when a boy. The place seemed to smile at me, and in a little while I began to feel tantalized and tormented that it was still the same, whereas I myself had undergone so many serious changes. (*PP* 201-02)

The feeling of being an outsider briefly melts away here, and Davies finds himself within the scene which seems to 'smile' back at him. This rare moment fulfills the longing that lies behind so much of his nature poetry, and undoes the distance and separation between person and natural scene that is implicit in the phrase 'stand and stare' from his best-known lines, 'What is this life if, full of care, / We have no time to stand and stare' (*SJ* 15). However, the feeling of being at one with the place is quickly replaced by a tormenting sense of the irremediable changes he has suffered since first enjoying the scene.

A journey gives this book a structure and prevents it from becoming just a string of disconnected anecdotes, like some of Davies's other prose memoirs. His reactions to being in Wales also provide a connecting thread. He notices that a song being sung in a pub is a Negro melody that he used to hear in the USA; and this is one of many moments when he is aware of time passing and things changing. He remembers his grandfather's habit of locking the house up against the wind; then, as if stirred by his own memories, recounts in moving detail his grandfather's death. These pages are uncharacteristically serious; for most of the book is in Davies's light manner. It ends with his trying to persuade a beggar whom he has met that he was once a beggar too.

In 1918 Davies met the artist William Nicholson who became a friend and regular illustrator of his books. In *Later Days* Davies describes him as 'a good fellow' with 'good stories of people and things' that he told with 'a clean tongue, too', enjoying particularly, rather like Davies, stories that went against himself (*LD* 184). They got on well and fantasised practical jokes, like dropping different coloured powders, red, green or black, in the Trafalgar Square fountains so they would seem to be 'spouting blood'. Another of their schemes was to 'wear rubber gloves with the palms smeared with fresh, red paint ... [and] visit certain houses ... of public men – and stamp a bloody hand on their front windows' (*LD* 185-6). Nicholson had reason for these slightly hysterical jokes, for during the war his wife had died, then his favourite son Anthony had been killed. Like Davies he was profoundly affected by the general suffering and depredations of the war, but unlike him he had 'a great fastidiousness in his manner of living', and an abhorrence of bohemianism with 'its implication of careless morals and slovenly habits' (*WN* 10), though like Davies he seems also to have made forays into the wild world of Augustus John and the Cafe Royal. Nicholson was a brilliant designer of posters, with his brother-in-law James Pryde, and of woodcuts. He illustrated books by W.E. Henley, Thomas Hardy, Siegfried Sassoon's *Memoirs of a Fox-hunting Man* (1929), and the second part of John Gay's *The Beggar's Opera*, *Polly*, in 1923 that prompted Davies to try his hand the same year, none too successfully, at his own beggar's opera, *True Travellers: A Tramp's Opera*. Davies's 1922 book, *The Hour of Magic* was decorated by Nicholson, as was *Moss and Feather* in 1928. Wit and elegance characterise the fine woodcuts and drawings that Nicholson executed for Davies's books. His 1927 portrait, now in the National Portrait Gallery, shows Davies in a walker's neckerchief, with amused, twinkling eyes and a face suffused with a barely suppressed smile. Nicholson drew Davies into his smart social world at Rottingdean, and Davies gave him insight into his milieu, telling him on one occasion that when he was poor 'and needed a woman [he] used to go down to Limehouse and have one of the cheap ones for a few pennies', but now that he was well enough off 'to go to Leicester Square or Piccadilly' he found his 'feet turning east as they used to do' (*WHDB* 56). Nicholson knew Davies as intimately as anyone, according to Stonesifer, and Davies felt free to tell stories against himself, like confessing to Nicholson that his dislike of de la Mare led him to practise pistol shooting using a picture of de la Mare as the target (*WHDB* 112). Their friendship was based on sociability and gossip, but also on deeper affinities. Nicholson's biographer has described her subject in terms that might apply just as well to Davies when she wrote that Nicholson was old-fashioned, and

> simply enchanted with the visual aspects of things he saw about him; they were enough to delight his eye and stimulate his creative ego. He neither read about nor talked of painting; his art was intuitive as far as art can ever be, and theorising was alien to him. (*WN* 27)

Davies's reputation continued to grow. His books, regularly issued by his publishers in fine editions, became collectors' items; and his poetry was appearing widely in anthologies, so that by 1918 nine volumes included his work (excluding the Georgian volumes), and by the time of his death in 1940 one hundred and three. By 1991 his bibliographer, Sylvia Harlow, was able to list two hundred and seven volumes with Davies poems in them.

Davies's 1918 volume of poems, *Forty New Poems*, shows his poetic powers at their height. It is imbued with signs of war, and touched with the madness that Davies said everyone felt at the time, including civilians. Georgian conventions are stretched to the limits, and a bit beyond, to express a wide range of subjects and feelings. The war's violence invades poems which seem to be conventional 'nature' poems. 'The Birds of Steel' has the poet remembering the sound of bees in an apple tree; but in the second stanza it surprisingly turns into the sound of mechanical warfare:

> I hear those bees again – ah no,
> It is the birds of steel, instead,
> Seeking their innocent prey below.

Georgian poetic conventions are distorted in order to represent these terrible, alien machines, grisly parodies of nature's flying creatures:

> Man-ridden birds of steel, unseen,
>   That come to drop their murdering lime
> On any child or harmless thing
>   Before the early morning time:
> Up, nearer God, they fly and sing. (*FNP* 48)

There's an undertone of violence through the whole volume, erupting where you might least expect it. 'On Hearing Mrs Woodhouse Play the Harpsichord' depends on the conceit that the poet fears that her music might make him dumb; it is imagined as a burst of mortar fire producing shell-shock, 'those great bursts that send my nerves / In waves to pound my heart away' (*FNP* 51). In 'England' the country is celebrated for not being one of climatic extremes or dangerous wildernesses; but the images draw on knowledge of the trenches: the line 'With bleeding mouths that freeze too hard to move' refers to cattle but might be soldiers at the front; and the next lines might be invoking a battle in France not an earthquake: 'No mountains here to spew their burning hearts / Into the valleys, on our human parts' (*FNP* 45). Even love poems, like 'Passion's Greed', have a violent intensity:

> Let me go burning to my death:
>   Nothing can come between our minds
> To ease me of this passion's greed:
>   We'll bite each other's necks like dogs,
> And ask our fingers if we bleed. (*FNP* 52)

In *Forty New Poems* the idea of nature, which is usually a conventional term denoting good, unbroken, purposeful activity, shows signs of breaking up under the weight of meaning it is supposed to carry. The social crisis of the war put Davies's idea of 'nature' under great pressure as a mode of representation. The only alternative to the war is bucolic escapism, a mode that would come to dominate Davies's poetic writing in the post-war years. 'Come, let us Find' imitates Christopher Marlowe to imagine an unreal place where the war will not penetrate:

Come, let us find a cottage, love,
  That's green for half a mile around;
To laugh at every grumbling bee,
  Whose sweetest blossom's not yet found ....

But we, away from our own kind,
  A different life can live and prove. (FNP 47

This comes close to the kind of writing that prompted Edith Sitwell, looking back on the Georgian poets in 1934, to exclaim against 'sub-Wordsworthian ideals' and 'advertisements of certain rustic parts of England' (*GP* 38). But Sitwell excluded Davies from her strictures, for, as Robert Ross notes, she was really condemning the Georgian trait of the pretence of emotion, and Davies wasn't guilty of that. Even so partisan a critic from the modernist wing as Ezra Pound had found much to praise in the 1916 *Collected Poems*, in particular his 'fine phrase and still finer simplicity', and the 'body of sound in these verses ... which ... many vers-librists might envy' (*P* 102). Pound's favourable comparison of Davies with modernist free-verse poets points to the fact that Davies had learned new techniques from modernist artists and writers. One reviewer of *Georgian Poetry 1918-1919* (which contained six poems from *Forty New Poems*) noticed the influence of modern painting in the desire 'to flash suddenly a light on a familiar thing from an unfamiliar angle' (*GP* 223). And Davies had also learned from Edward Thomas's *Poems* of 1917 a spareness of style that Thomas himself had acquired from the Symbolists and Imagists. Had Davies taken further the modernist tendencies of *Forty New Poems* he would have become another sort of poet altogether. As it turned out, he reverted to a version of Georgianism that was to become increasingly outmoded as the years passed.

By the end of the war Davies had got to know many of London's artistic and literary luminaries. He had met the Sitwells, Osbert, Sacheverell and Edith, and through them he met Aldous Huxley and others. The young poet Richard Church, whom he met in 1918, became a friend and one of his most sympathetic early critics. Conrad Aiken was another young poet whom Davies befriended, and was to be a witness at Davies's and Helen Payne's wedding in 1923. Stonesifer suggests that while Davies was certainly generous and supportive of these young writers, he was also glad to enjoy in their friendship a respite from the jealousy he was sure some established writers felt for him; an insecurity that was mixed with pride, for he now regarded himself 'as one of England's leading poets' (*WHDB* 109). He was extremely jealous of de la Mare, disliked John Masefield, especially after he became Poet Laureate in 1930, and considered Yeats another of his poetic rivals. Stonesifer reports the sly, amusing line that Davies would use about his supposed rivals, asking his interlocutor if it had ever occurred to him that when people spoke of Yeats they said what a great poet he was, but when they spoke of de la Mare (or some other contemporary) they said what a charming man. William Nicholson saw evidence of Davies's serio-comic rivalries in his list of contemporary poets who, when they offended him in some way, were struck off one by one. By the time he saw the list only Robert Graves and Davies himself remained on it. The artist Laura Knight said of Davies's sensitivity that he 'always ... had a bare toe stuck out ready to be trodden on' (*WHDB* 113). Davies's professional insecurities were an extension of his social fears, deriving no doubt from his working-class background and his years as a beggar. When he was on holiday with Laura and Harold Knight in Cornwall in 1922 he was wary of visiting the pub in the village, telling the Knights that he could not be sure who might see him in the pub or coming out of it, saying, 'I've got to be very careful with my Civil Pension' (*CM* 286). Laura Knight's 1920 drawing of Davies captures the vulnerability and suspicion in his personality.

Georgian poetry's penultimate collection published in 1919, *Georgian Poetry 1918-1919*, elicited from critics increasing expressions of disapproval from which Davies was not exempt. The *Manchester Guardian* saw 'an unexhaustible vein of gold' in de la Mare's and Davies's poems; but the *Daily Herald* thought that the selection from Davies, 'one of the few living poets whom nearly everyone accepts', was 'unsatisfactory to many' (*GP* 281, 294). Holbrook Jackson indicated precisely why people were turning away from Georgianism when he wrote in *Today* that the freshness had departed, and that 'the particular vein has exhausted itself ... There is a younger generation and a newer poetry' (*GP* 312). Dwindling sales reflected dwindling interest. The important ideological function that the

Georgian volumes had performed during the war, of sustaining an image of a peaceful country and supporting a set of values in opposition to the degradations of war, was no longer necessary after 1918. Georgian poetry could be read in a negative way as a kind of war poetry, embodying values from the pre-war years that sustained readers in the face of wartime destruction. But once the war was over the world that emerged was found to have changed, and the values of Georgian poetry to have become anachronistic.

It seems that an unhappy love affair may have contributed to Davies's leaving Sevenoaks in 1914. In 1918 another equally obscure attempt at a permanent relationship with a woman ended in failure when he broke off an engagement to marry a woman from Wales. The engagement ended when, according to one report, he visited the woman's home and discovered her acting cruelly towards her father. Davies's personal situation in these post-war years was made more unhappy by the fact that his mother had ended up in a Newport workhouse and he could not afford to help her. He was himself too ill at the time to travel to Wales, and she died without his being able to see her. Laura Knight remembers as Davies's greatest source of grief his inability to provide relief for his mother.

Laura Knight provides an image of Davies as a close and likeable friend. She and her husband Harold Knight, also a painter, met Davies through a mutual friend at the Cafe Royal and visited him for tea at his Great Russell Street rooms. She was struck by his eyes, and amused when Davies insisted that her husband paint him so as to make the most of them: 'It's by my eyes people know me as a poet', he claimed (*CM* 284). He was vain too about his hair and would cut it meticulously with a pair of nail scissors 'a tuft at a time ... clipped off as close as possible, except in front where an imposing upright twist was carefully trimmed' (*CM* 287). Laura Knight's memories of Davies on holiday with them and other friends at Lamora in Cornwall, the place discovered by Augustus John, shows him revelling in his camping skills acquired as a tramp in America, but also as a rather solitary figure on the edge of this artists' colony, attentive to his own unusual, powerful feelings. She remembers him in charge of the nightly campfire, 'all aglow with fire-light, sweat, toil, and pride, with a long, strong, and straight branch in hand, as a master triumphant' feeding and retrimming the blaze. Davies was also greatly affected by the valley where they stayed, and deeply fearful of sleeping alone in his hut at night; but quite of what it was impossible for his friends to say. He defended himself against emotional hurt from other people because, as he said, by getting 'too fond of people, one is apt to get mixed up with their troubles and when they die one grieves'. Laura Knight understood the source of Davies's uncertainties, seeing him as unable to understand how other people might think or act, and, in trying to understand them, seizing 'on some trifling feature of a man's make-up on which to build his whole judgement' (*CM* 288-91). This shrewd judgement catches the individualism of Davies's responses, which were ideal building blocks for his lyric poems but also the source of his personal isolation. It also suggests the source of his prose technique which proceeds from one quirky observation to the next; and also why he was well advised to avoid extended analytical writing. Unfortunately, in his 1920 volume of poems, *The Song of Life*, he allowed himself to lapse into philosophising.

This volume, with a frontispiece from a painting of Davies by Laura Knight, was not well received. The fifty-eight four-line stanzas of the title poem are an ill-judged attempt by Davies to generalise his reactions to life, and are often as weak as this one:

> Aye, even now, when I sit here alone,
> I feel the breath of that strange terror near;
> But as my mind has not sufficient strength
> To give it shape or form or any kind,
> I turn to the things I know, and banish fear. (*SL* 51)

In the book Davies seems to be casting round with some difficulty for distinct poetic voices to express the conflicting reactions that the end of the war brought. In 'The Coming of Peace' the social realism of the poet's involvement in celebrations jars incongruously with his bucolic reference to a cuckoo:

> And as I moved amidst that silent multitude,
>   Feeling the presence of a wild excitement there,
> The world appeared to me so strange and wonderful –
> I almost heard a cuckoo in Trafalgar Square! (*SL* 22)

Although Davies deployed images of nature as disjointed and comfortless to express social distress in *Forty New Poems*, here the conventional cuckoo is comically inadequate to suggest this particular moment's being 'strange and wonderful'. There are a lot of birds in this book, including several imaginary ones in incongruous places.

A few of the poems do contain vigorous ideas and language, and Davies's characteristic enjoyment of physicality. 'You Interfering Ladies' is directed at those who would repress the lower orders in the name of moral improvement:

> Let beggars, who'll not wash with soap,
> > Enjoy their scratching till they bleed:
> Let all poor women, if they please,
> Enjoy a pinch of snuff, and sneeze. (*SL* 43)

But as if in recognition of the direction his writing would follow for the rest of his career, and the kind of poems that would find a ready paying public, he writes in 'The Mint' of his thoughts being 'coins, on which I live', and the dies which 'stamp [his] thoughts' as being 'Trees, blossoms, birds, and children' (*SL* 36)

Davies's financial position, in fact, became more secure when, first, in 1920 his Civil List pension was raised to £150 per annum, and, second, Jonathan Cape became his publisher on the retirement of A.C. Fifield. Immediately Cape began reissuing Davies's earlier books in cheap editions, laying the groundwork for Davies to become a popular poet. Davies at this time was willing to try his hand at any new literary ventures that presented themselves, and in October 1921 took on the unlikely task of literary editorship of the magazine *Form*, with A.O. Spare as his fellow editor. This magazine only survived for three numbers even though Davies was able to call on his artist contacts to provide copy, such as William Nicholson who provided a drawing for the second number. The unintellectual Davies was an unsuitable editor, forced, according to Robert Graves, to become pompous from embarrassment, and the venture simply sank. Less unsuccessful was his editing *Shorter Lyrics of the Twentieth-Century 1900-1922* for publication by the Poetry Bookshop in 1922, for he had wide knowledge of lyric poetry. He was to edit another anthology, *Jewels of Song:An Anthology of Short Poems* in 1930 for Cape, launched on his own established reputation as a lyric poet.

The post-war years saw Davies continuing his socialising with the literary panjandrums of London. Arnold Bennett was at a dinner party of the Sitwells in 1919 along with Lytton Strachey, Leonard Woolf, Robert Nichols, Siegfried Sassoon, Aldous Huxley, W.J. Turner, Herbert Read and Davies, whom he noted in his diary he liked. In 1921 Davies moved to new rooms at 13 Avery Row, Brook Street, where his first year was marked by long periods of illness that he called at the time rheumatism but later revealed to be venereal disease. The misery and weakness he suffered in Avery Row during 1922 was graphically described in *Young Emma*, not published until 1980 after his death and the death of the woman he was to marry, Helen Payne. His relationship with this young woman, almost thirty years his junior, was to transform the last twenty years of his life.

1. Sailing ships by a timber slip at Newport Old Town Docks, c.1892.

2. W.H. Davies, aged 37, the frontispiece of his third collection, *Nature Poems and Others*, 1908.

3. Portrait of W.H. Davies, aged 45, in pencil on brown paper, by William
Rothenstein, 1916, the most romanticised image of Davies there is. A blander
collotype of it appeared as the frontispiece of *Collected Poems: First Series*, 1916.

Love's Caution

Tell them, when you are home again,
　How warm the air was now;
How silent were the birds and leaves,
　And of the moon's full glow;
　　And how we saw afar
　　A falling star:
It was a tear of pure delight
Ran down the face of Heaven this happy night.

Our kisses are but love in flower,
　Until that greater time
When, gathering strength, those flowers take wing,
　And Love can reach his prime.
　　And now, my heart's delight,
　　Good night, good night;
Give me the last sweet kiss —
But do not breathe at home one word of this!

　　　　　　W. H. Davies.

(4)

4. Manuscript of 'Love's Caution' in Davies's small, neat handwriting, first published in *The Song of Life and Other Poems*, 1920.

5. An illustration by Davies's friend William Nicholson for *The Hour of Magic and Other Poems*, 1922. It shows Davies asleep with the images in his mind hovering overhead.

7. A fanciful illustration by William Nicholson, of a beetle appearing to beg by selling shoe laces, for *True Travellers: A Tramp's Opera in Three Acts*, 1923.

6. Illustration by William Nicholson of a tramp resembling Davies for *True Travellers: A Tramp's Opera in Three Acts*, 1923; a libretto which was never staged.

8. W.H. Davies and his wife Helen photographed in the Gloucestershire town of Nailsworth in 1935, where they lived in various houses from around 1929 to Davies's death in 1940.

9. Davies receives public recognition from his home town of Newport as he and the Mayor pose (with unknown child) outside Church House Inn, sometime in the 1930s.

10. W.H. Davies, aged 67, receiving congratulations from the Mayoress of Newport in September 1938 at the unveiling of a plaque on Church House Inn where Davies claimed to have been born. Also in the photograph are the Poet Laureate, John Masefield, whom Davies disliked, and Davies's wife.

Six: Love, Marriage and
Final Years 1922-1940

It was one of Davies's women friends, Laura Knight, who spotted how his pride in being a beggar and his sexual pride were linked: being a master beggar 'was part of the game', she was to write, and 'the brilliant eyes with their long lashes made an appeal which women found hard to resist' (*OP* 240). The *Autobiography of a Super-Tramp* relates with self-satisfaction how he would beg generous quantities of fine food from American housewives. A man begging from a woman is a supplicant, hoping that his personal appeal will prompt her response; he is powerless, while she has the power to deny or fulfill his request. Begging for money or food transposes to the material plane the begging for love of the medieval and renaissance Petrarchan lover; and Davies had read enough Elizabethan love poetry to know how it represented relations between women and men. His love poetry sometimes represents idealised, fleeting encounters modelled on the kind of hopeless love found in early English love poetry, or offers women as powerful and unattainable. 'A Lovely Woman' of 1908 expresses the sense of women's erotic power and otherness from its opening lines, 'Now I can see what Helen was: / Men cannot see this woman pass / And be not stirred'; and creates a string of images of desire rather than fulfilment from scraps of literary tradition:

> She seemed as sent to our cold race
> For fear the beauty of her face
> Made Paradise in flames like Troy –
> I could have gazed all day with joy. (*NatP* 46)

However, some of the other ways in which he imagines love of women are very different from this Petrarchanism. In 'Jenny' and 'A

Maiden and her Hair', also from *Nature Poems*, the girls are unattainable only because the intense sexual love they provide gives
them mysterious and distant power, or because they flit from lover
to lover, though that causes pain:

> Ah, Jenny's gone, I know not where;
>   Her face I cannot hope to see;
> And every time I think of her
>   The world seems one big grave to me. (*NatP* 14)

However, the poet often turns away from the idea of a permanent
love for woman and asserts that solitary self-sufficiency will protect
him from the pain love leads to. In 'The Wanderer' from *The Bird of
Paradise* of 1914 he fantasises himself as wandering alone:

> For, free, he lives his simple life,
> And has not risked it with a wife....
> Has studied his own self, to find
> His best friends fancies of the mind. (*BP* 53)

That chilling idea seems to have shaped Davies's relationships with
women through most of his adult life. Sex for him usually meant
sexual freedom, though it could also suggest the playful or foolish,
as when he mocks his own fetish for women's luxuriant hair in
'Where She is Now':

> O that I could leap forward now,
>   Behind her back and, with my lips,
> Break through those curls above her nape,
>   That hover close and lightly there. (*TO* 41-2)

Davies can convey both the physical reality and the spiritual
force of sexual desire, its sudden intensities and its infantile ambiva-
lence, as 'The Bee Lover' of 1933 illustrates:

> He comes with a song,
>   This gallant young lover,
> And he fusses about
>   Till his passion is over:
> Till he lies like a baby –
>   With love in a mist –

To dribble and sleep
  On the face he has kissed. (*MG* 52)

The True Traveller (1912) contains accounts of his relationships with prostitutes when he was on the road, and *Young Emma*, which he wrote in 1924, is a candid account of not just his sexual relationships in immediately post-war London but also of the conventions of sexual behaviour among a section of poor urban women that is very far from idealised. When Davies turned fifty in 1920 he wanted to change his sexual life, with its string of mistresses and casual encounters, and find a wife. It was not until 1922 when he found Helen Payne that he was able to reconcile two aspects of his sexual feelings, the desire for a woman as an idealised erotic object, and for a woman with whom he could establish a stable, practical arrangement for living together.

Young Emma provides the only source for Davies's love affair and marriage. When she was his lover, the twenty-odd year old Helen Payne, called Emma in Davies' account, remained out of sight or unnoticed by his friends, none of whom record memories of her. The transformations that were taking place in Davies were intimate and secret, and involved him disappearing from London with his new lover at the end of 1922, and beginning a life that brought to an end his involvement with a wide acquaintance of writers and artists, and his mingling with high society. By 1920 Davies was tiring of London, as Helen Thomas, Edward Thomas's widow, realised, noticing that 'Davies became as bored with them as they with him' (*TA* 90). While it is unnecessary to assume that the stories told in *Young Emma* are absolutely accurate, their effect is persuasively authentic. Davies tells of his relationships first with Bella then with Louise who are 'mistresses' of a peculiar kind, part prostitute, part cook and companion, who live with him. Such temporary partnerships are pragmatic not romantic. When Davies first meets Louise she is living with another man but 'looking for a chance to change her lovers, if she could find one to her liking' (*YE* 36). In Davies's words, the arrangement means the woman has 'to look after my comfort' in return for finding 'a kind and easy master' (*YE* 62). Davies's capacity to write about these intimacies, prohibited at the time in respectable literature, is proof of his mind's independence from prevailing conventions. He wrote

Young Emma shortly after the events the book describes, and indeed he sometimes writes as if the act of writing were prompting a re-experiencing of what is recounted. The following passage shows confession and recollection strangely combined:

> I was dressed smartly in a light overcoat, which was almost new, and it was this that probably made a number of women smile and come to a very slow walk, to enable me to make the next advance. But here I must make another confession which may appear strange indeed. It is this – I am a very shy man. For instance, if one of these women did not actually come to a dead halt and speak to me first, it was not at all likely that I would have turned back and followed her, however much I might have been impressed by her beauty, and however cordial might have been her greeting. Time after time have I gone out looking for a woman, and time after time have I returned home alone, because I have not had the courage to take advantage of a woman's encouragement. (*YE* 56)

The core of the story of *Young Emma* lies in Davies's decision at the age of fifty 'to trouble no more about respectable women, but to find a wife in the common streets' (*YE* 22). The story is strange but, as with the *Autobiography*, its strangeness disappears in the way Davies simply takes for granted that what he writes about is, as he says, 'pure'. He explains his decision to seek a wife in the streets by saying that literary peoples' lives seemed so far away from him, that it appeared much more natural for me to seek a wife among the kind of people I knew before I was thirty years of age than the ones I knew later' (*YE* 23). One night he goes out on his 'old quest' and meets Emma on the Edgware Road:

> All at once a bus stopped right in front of me, and I looked, half wondering what kind of passengers would alight. There was only one; and that was a young girl who could be anything between fifteen and twenty years of age. Thinking of her youth, I began to turn my eyes away, but the smile on her face would not allow me to dismiss my interest in that way. Not only that, but it soon became obvious that the smile was meant for me. If I had any doubt, it was to go at once, for, in passing close by, she nodded slightly, and almost came to a halt .... However, when she turned her head and saw that I was not following her, she, apparently

liking my appearance too well to lose me, stood looking my way, and waiting to see what I intended to do. (*YE* 57)

He takes her home and she becomes his mistress and housekeeper. Some time later he finds he has a serious venereal disease, and fears that his new lover has infected him. During his illness Emma herself is suddenly taken ill, and Davies describes in nightmarish detail the events of the night which he merely mentions in *Later Days*, when he is lying sick and helpless, and she is crying out in pain in the room below, and no one is able to find a doctor who will visit her or a hospital to take her in. That night Emma miscarries a six-month old foetus. The crisis of their mutual helplessness and suffering is a turning-point for Davies. One uncanny detail, mentioned in passing, gives the account a real sense of horror and disorientation: 'Strange to say, it did not occur to me to send for my own doctor, and hers too' (*YE* 80).

As this crisis is recounted, the writing becomes charged with images of violence, death, and the desire for death: 'My capacity for taking punishment', Davies writes,

> has been tremendous, but the spirit to inflict it on another was not given to me at birth. But in this new life to come, ... [it is I that will be the hunter] ... it will be the decree of the gods that I shall ride on the backs of my enemies. (*YE* 89)

The language of violence confirms one critic's view that 'at the bottom of Davies's mind there was a ground of horror, a recognition he seldom or never expressed in verse' (*HMP* 221). *Young Emma* articulates that ground of horror. His life endangered by a disease he thinks he has contracted from Emma, he nevertheless cannot bring himself to stop being her lover and yet cannot talk to this innocent girl about the situation. His whole existence hangs in the balance between being saved by a love he is unsure of, or doomed by a disease she is unwittingly carrying. The book records the almost unbearable moral and physical strains that Davies suffers.

The events are recounted from Davies's point of view with the outcome withheld from the reader. Retracing the path of Davies's shocks and bafflement as we read, we depend for our understanding on his conjectures. When he is reinfected he again blames Emma;

and his account of entering their bedroom after the quarrel that follows this discovery takes him to what he later describes as the brink of a *crime passionel* –

> I thought that young Emma had not been to sleep at all and, hearing my accidental movement, got the impression that I had come to murder her .... It was a most horrible thought to have, for I, of course, had never once had the least intention of doing her any harm. The only likelihood there was of my doing that would be if I went mad, and did what all mad people do – attack the one I loved most' (*YE* 128-29).

The prose here suggests profound passion, as the best poetry does, though the feelings here are conflicted. Profound feeling cast in a simple style compels the reader to respond.

The account ends with startling suddenness: she is healthy, he was the infected one, he had failed to see the obvious truth that an earlier lover caused his disease. The sense of this ending is that the whole story of desire, silence, bafflement, fear and anger is the protagonist's spiritual struggle simply to discover Emma's love for him as being real. The external events that Davies records are underdetermined, but the emotional plot emerges convincingly. Like a Freudian case-history, the story depends on trivial or even imagined events, and appeals to a deep logic behind the verbal screen of the text. But *Young Emma* makes for uncanny reading, for the reader senses that Davies himself is not in control of the significance of his powerful material.

If it is true, as Starobinski believes, that autobiography is always the story of 'conversion, entry into a new life, the operation of Grace' (*SA* 78), then *Young Emma* is certainly autobiographical. The ultimate turn of the protagonist's mind is towards a revelation of the truth:

> That night, when I was lying quietly in bed, I went over the whole thing, from beginning to end; and the more I thought of it, the more horrible it became. For instance, if this poor girl, who was now sleeping at my side, had only realised the meaning of my charge against her, and my reproach, she would have left me long ago, that was certain .... It was strange that I never once suspected the real author of my trouble; that the woman with the silk stockings was the cause of it all (*YE* 154).

The signs had been obvious but he travels a hard and circuitous route before he can finally see this simple truth. This is a romance narrative with the discovery of a woman's love as its destination.

As this account suggests, this is the most extraordinary of Davies's prose books. It is written with a subjective intensity quite unlike the ironical, detached point of view of the *Autobiography* and the other memoirs. It was written between Davies's marrying Helen Payne in February 1923 and submitting the manuscript to Jonathan Cape in September 1924, when the impact of the emotional trauma he had just been living through made itself felt in what he wrote. By the time he wrote to Cape he was already having cold feet, telling him that it would have to be published 'under the name "Anonymous"', and adding, 'It frightens me now it is done' (*YE* 9). Cape sent the manuscript to George Bernard Shaw, and Shaw wrote in reply, marking the letter 'Very Private', that it was as amazing a document as the *Autobiography*, the record of

> a fully–developed, vigorous, courageous, imaginative, and specifically talented adult, with plenty of experience of civilized life in the best literary and other society in London, and with the outlook of a slum boy of six or seven (*YE* 157).

He advised that Davies should not publish it on two grounds: firstly it would harm him by showing how alien he actually was from the literary and social world that he had been taken up by, and secondly because it would give away his wife. Meanwhile, Davies had told his wife about the book and she was 'very much alarmed'. He wrote to Cape,

> As she is only 24 years of age and has every prospect of outliving us all I have come to the conclusion that the MS. must be destroyed and not get into the hands of strangers in about 50 years' time from now.

He asked Cape to return the manuscript and let him know that they had destroyed the two typewritten copies, for otherwise his mind could never be at rest. 'Please don't try to persuade me to do anything different', he concluded, 'as a book that is not fit to be published now can never be fit' (*YE* 11). Cape did return the manuscript but wrote saying that he would delay destroying the copies in case Davies on reflection considered that to be too drastic. The next week Davies replied, telling Cape that he had received the manuscript and was already making use of some of its material (in what was to become *Later Days*), and telling Cape to 'destroy the two typewritten copies as soon as you like' (*YE* 11). Davies made no further inquiry as to the fate of the typescripts. Cape placed them in a safe, from which they emerged in 1940 after Davies's death, remaining unpublished because Mrs Davies was still alive; and again in 1972 when the publisher decided that the book could appear but only after Mrs Davies's death. Helen Matilda Davies died in 1979 and *Young Emma* was published the next year. It included a foreword by C.V. Wedgewood, who in 1940 had been working as a reader for Cape and read the typescript, in which she surmised that Davies may have half-consciously wished the book to survive, for his final instructions to Cape were quite weak and ambiguous – destroy the copies 'as soon as you like' – and no attempt was made to ensure they had been carried out. In any case, ignoring Davies's request meant the survival of his most remarkable book.

'Stings', from *Love Poems* of 1935, recalls Davies's meeting with his wife in more tranquil terms than those of *Young Emma*, though the old-fashioned romantic diction is jolted by the direct assertion of the last line:

> Can I forget your coming, like the Moon
>   When, robed in light, alone, without a star,
> She visits ruins; and the peace you brought,
>   When I with all the world was still at war. (*LP* 48)

The metaphor of his lover as a star is the same as he used many years before to represent the dead lover of his youth in Wales.

The 1922 volume of poems *The Hour of Magic*, technically assured verse with decorations by William Nicholson, showed no signs of the love affair though it is concerned with women's lives. The lives of working-class city women are recorded in 'Two Women', the mother who saw a male child beaten by the midwife as it is born, and the wife who suffers beatings from the same male when he's an adult: 'he's not worth the skin – / As husband, father, or a son – /

That he was made for living in' (*HM* 6). 'A Woman's History' is another sardonic tale of a woman's life glimpsed through incidents between the ages of five and seventy-five, by which time the old woman is heartless and cruel: 'She, active, strong, and full of breath, / Has caught the cat that stole an eel, / And beaten it to death' (*HM* 29). 'Pastures' strikes quite another feeling in its celebration of love-making as innocent and infantile, a feeling intensified by its 'young lambs' and nursery rhymes:

> I know a pasture twice as sweet,
>   Although I may not show't;
> Where my five fingers go each night
>   To nibble, like you sheep,
> All over my love's breast, and there
>   Lie down to sleep. (*HM* 8)

November 1922 also saw the publication of the fifth and final volume of *Georgian Poetry 1920-1922* in which Davies had five poems, all but one from *The Song of Life*. The collection as a whole was met with considerable criticism, though once again Davies's poems were exempted from the harshest of this because critics recognised their authenticity despite occasional banalities. Davies though was writing in the style, essentially Georgian, that he was to maintain until his death. The Georgian mode that in 1912 and 1915 had 'implied vigour, revolt, and youth' by 1917 had come to suggest 'retrenchment, escape, and enervation' (*GR* 187). In a striking historical conjunction, the fifth Georgian volume came out one month after the first issue of *The Criterion* which contained T.S. Eliot's *The Waste Land*. Clearly, seismic shifts were happening in culture, and in the ways in which the contemporary world could be understood. Davies was completely cut off from these changes both imaginatively and physically, for he left London with Helen Payne to live in East Grinstead, Sussex in late 1922. His seclusion did not protect him, however, from another kind of criticism in J.C. Squire's parodies of 1921 which infuriated him. It is not easy to parody Davies's brand of artful simplicity that challenges the reader not to turn aside with a sophisticated sneer but to recognise the validity of what's being said, however slight it may appear. You might even see this tactical simplicity, or even banality, as part of Davies's defence against his class 'superiors' and their taste and manners. He claimed, for example, that he found it difficult to talk to society ladies because he could not 'hold [his] water long enough for prolonged conversation' (*PW* 39). Squire's parodies sneer at writing that is outside middle-class educated norms, not just at simple style:

> I'm sure that you would never guess
> The tales I hear from birds and flowers,
> Without them sure 'twould be a mess
> I'd make of all the summer hours;
> But these fair things they make for me
> A lovely life of joy and glee.

It would be hard for any parodist to equal the silliness of some of the actual lines in *Georgian Poetry 1920-1922*, such as these from a contributor named Kerr: 'I lingered at a gate and talked / A little with a lonely lamb.' While Georgianism had certainly dwindled to insignificance in the cultural scene, it was the mode that Davies, having practised over the years, had brought to some polish and completeness, and was to stick to in the years ahead. The inevitable result was that he became a less and less significant writer in national terms, though he remained popular with a loyal following of readers who were happy to read unfashionable and outmoded poetry.

Helen Payne and William Davies were married in February 1923 at the East Grinstead Registry Office, with Davies's young friends Conrad Aiken and Martin Armstrong as witnesses. In his fifty-third year Davies had at last achieved what he had longed for for so long, a home. At the ceremony he was extremely nervous, and made his wife-to-be nervous too. Their meeting with the witnesses was strained, and Davies's near panic was not helped when he wrote his wife's middle name wrongly in the register. At last they returned to the Davies' house and enjoyed a wedding breakfast of port and sweet cake. The marriage was to mark a break with Davies's old London life, and many old friendships faded away from this moment. The married pair formed an intimate, private relationship. She called him 'Bunny' and he called her 'Dinah'. Curiously, he had used that name once before in the *Autobiography* in referring to 'poor black Dinah' who so much coveted flimsy muslin from her master's store (*AST* 107), a usage which suggests tenderness and pity for an oppressed woman, in this case racially oppressed. Perhaps he had similar feelings for the vulnerable, pregnant young woman he picked up in the street. But in any case, once they were married it seems that Helen Davies began to be more assertive.

The marriage of Davies and Helen Payne was not based on liberal principles, like those the Bloomsbury circle were living by in the 1920s. On the contrary, the marriage was based on the values of Davies's working-class boyhood. In *Young Emma* he explicitly turns to class when he attributes his occasional outbursts at 'Emma' of 'vulgar words, like those of a bully' to his coming from 'the common people'. He behaves like this, he writes, despite his 'association with people of more culture'. Luckily, however, 'Emma' reacts to his outbursts with more amusement than fear, because she too comes 'from the common people' and so finds 'blunt words and open anger' perfectly natural (*YE* 125). He decided that he could not marry a 'respectable woman', because such women bored him with 'their long, lifeless talk on books and art'; instead his wife must come from 'the common streets' (*YE* 22-3). The relations between this husband and wife are demarcated along traditional lines. She understands nothing about his work and leaves him entirely free to follow 'what was the greatest joy in [his] life'. He never wanted anyone, he wrote, 'to share [his] literary dream'. So his new wife suits him because she is neither a 'brilliant talker' nor 'a great brain' but rather 'a great heart and an affectionate spirit' (*YE* 119). Helen Davies soon claimed a working-class wife's authority to establish rules of respectability and to regulate the behaviour of her husband. She disapproved of his drinking, and especially drinking in pubs. His visits to London were curtailed with the result that some old friendships disappeared. And his sexual adventuring was brought to an end. There were losses for Davies in his new domestic happiness; no more visits to the theatre and the music-hall that he enjoyed so much, less gossip about his friends and their lives; no more glamorous dinner parties with the upper classes nor wild parties with the bohemians of Fitzrovia.

But Davies was happy to give up the London life he had become increasingly tired of. His recompense was the achieving of a private, even secretive, domestic intimacy. When 'Emma' had been in hospital she wrote to Davies telling him how she was, but adding two phrases that revealed her trust and affection for him and that gave him the courage to pursue the relationship. She wrote that she was 'longing to be home', a notion that had peculiar poignancy for him; and, more surprisingly perhaps, 'tucked away in the left-hand corner ... one word, to stand all by itself ... the word "Bunnykins"' (*YE* 96). The prospect of achieving a 'home' after so many years was at last about to be realised, as well as emotional and sexual intimacy with a woman whom he felt he could trust, which had also seemed for so long an impossibility. His emotional distrust was no doubt heightened by his awareness of his physical disability; but he had chosen a partner whose vulnerabilities balanced his own: she was a young woman from the working class, degraded by her pregnancy by her middle-class employer; and forced to walk the streets in search of men to protect her. Her nickname for him suggests the element of childlike conspiracy in their mutual love, and the creation of a world in which they were the only inhabitants. Certainly, Davies's Welsh relations did not attend their wedding or visit the couple after they had moved to Gloucestershire, for they disapproved of the match between the fifty-two year old husband and his twenty-three year old wife. Whatever the world thought, however, Davies's marriage to Helen Payne was a transforming moment equivalent in its impact on the direction of Davies's life to the moment when his first book of poetry, *The Soul's Destroyer*, was published in March 1905. These two moments are the climaxes of Davies's two autobiographies, and each concerns self-transformation, in the *Autobiography* from drifter and destitute to writer, and in *Young Emma* from lonely bachelor to ardent husband. Like his friend Edward Thomas, who transformed himself from an overworked literary hack into a fine poet, Davies remade himself – twice. The *Autobiography* and *Young Emma*, taken together, trace the fulfillment of a personal destiny. Ironically, the path his life follows is from the extraordinary to the ordinary: from social marginal to happy husband. And as his life became conventional and happier, so his writing became less interesting. Life and writing seem to have been intimately intertwined in Davies, but in these autobiographical books, as in his best poetry, they combine, perhaps fortuitously, but certainly productively. The responsiveness to experience as the basis for writing, links the prose life-writings with the poetry.

Davies was willing to turn his hand to forms of writing other than poetry. In 1923, in the wake of the theatrical success of Nigel Playfair's productions at the Hammersmith Lyric Theatre of Gay's eighteenth-century ballad opera *The Beggar's Opera*, and its sequel *Polly*, Davies wrote the libretto for a similar low-life opera which he called *True Travellers: A Tramp's Opera*. Davies was editor of the ill-fated *Form* at the time he wrote the libretto, and during these few months he was fired by thoughts of expanding literary accomplishment and fame. But he was self-deluded to imagine success flowing from either of these ventures. On 1 February 1923 he wrote to Clifford Bax, who had been involved with *Polly*, about collaborating with him on the opera, and mentioning Frederic Austin as a possible composer and Playfair as producer. Bax agreed to read the piece, and then received another letter from Davies saying, in some desperation, that he did not care 'who does the music, [or] who acts in it, or who produces it' 'if the opera can be produced', though he did want William Nicholson to design the scenery (*SIKW* 68).But Bax found the piece 'unactable', as did Playfair, and that was the end of Davies's theatrical ambitions. The plot of *True Travellers* is as flimsy as its characterisation, and theatre-lovers would only have marvelled 'at the absurdity of the rest of it' (*WHDB* 140). Presumably Davies believed that his direct experience of living as a tramp would provide the piece's interest. But the subtle tones and points of view of his prose accounts of tramping were unsuited to a theatrical form like Gay's that required 'complete sophistication and artificiality' (*WHDB* 140). Bax's conclusion about this episode, that Davies 'was not the man for any sustained flight' was not one that Davies himself found easy to accept. But all was not lost for in October 1923 Jonathan Cape turned the dud libretto into a marketable item by producing it with fine line drawings and decorations by Nicholson and turning it into one of Davies's most handsome books. It did also contain some stylish short lyrics, smooth, technically assured and individual, such as the strongly erotic 'Around that Waist':

> To feel her soft round body slip and turn,

And still to feel no bones; that clings to me,
Till she becomes at last the trembling flower
  Kissed without mercy by a powerful bee. (*TO* 75)

Cape was assiduous in promoting Davies by supporting the publication of a flow of books from him as well as reprinting his old
volumes; and it was largely thanks to these efforts that Davies
remained in the public eye as a living author. Davies's income
increased as a result of all this, a welcome change for a man very
conscious of the financial responsibilities of marriage. A second
Collected Poems was published in April 1923, with Augustus John's
portrait as frontispiece; and then a *Selected Poems* in December of the
same year. *Secrets*, a new volume of poems, appeared in April 1924,
and *A Poet's Alphabet* in October 1925, the gap, relatively long for
Davies and Cape, caused by the writing and ultimate rejection of
Young Emma. Despite this, Cape prompted Davies to try writing
more autobiography, and this time the outcome was *Later Days* published in October 1925. Meanwhile Davies was succeeding with
short flights of prose, such as articles for periodicals, such as 'What
I Gained and Lost by Not Staying at School' for *Teachers World* of
June 1923, and introductions to editions of other writers, like *Moll
Flanders* in 1924, the *Augustan Book of Poetry*, *Burns's Poetical Works*,
and *The Adventures of a Scholar Tramp*, all in 1925. While these introductions show Davies's talent for a new, minor kind of writing, the
subjects of the books he wrote about all returned him to the fact of
his once having been a tramp and beggar, and kept that unchanging
image before the public as his trademark, however much he may
have wished to leave it behind.

Meanwhile, in East Grinstead, domestic life was establishing its
hold over the recently married couple. Davies's habit was to retire to
his study every day except Sunday and 'wait on inspiration'; and,
when it came, record its effusions in his tiny handwriting no bigger,
according to his friend Brian Waters, 'than the type on this printed
page' (*EWHD* 14). Helen Davies was even shyer than Davies himself
and hated meeting strangers. The couple's sociability was severely
restricted, especially as Davies's relatives in Wales would have
nothing to do with this scandalous marriage, and Helen Davies's relatives seem not to have maintained close contact with her. She was

happy housekeeping and gardening for her 'Bunnikins' whom she kept close by her as much as she could, and discouraged from staying away overnight to visit friends in London. Davies's London life quickly withered and was left behind. He writes about it in *Later Days* as something that is now in the past. Laura Knight remembered the sorrow she and her husband felt when, after Davies's marriage, 'then our ways parted' (*CM* 292). In 1926 a friend of Davies's thought that he wished to move nearer to London than East Grinstead, for much as Davies loved the countryside, and wrote poetry about it, he also enjoyed the pleasures of city life; but his wife, herself brought up in the country near East Grinstead, preferred life there. Davies had a lifelong love of the theatre from his boyhood in Newport, and another old friend recalled tracking him down one night to the London Palladium where he saw him in the front row of the gallery 'smoking his clay pipe and laughing outrageously at a comedian' (*WEW* 171). Davies had to resign himself to a quieter life in East Grinstead, apparently believing that such limitations were the natural condition of all marriages. Curiously, although Davies dearly loved his wife, her strict regime returned him to a regime rather like that of his grandmother's, against which he so chafed when he was a boy. Certainly Davies and his wife quarrelled as they edged towards finding a *modus vivendi*, but his only known rebellion was after they moved to Nailsworth where he would wave at the girls in a nearby laundry. The independence that he had defended so fiercely all his life was finally yielded for a marriage based on domestic intimacy and withdrawal from the world.

Davies's last seventeen years brought him personal happiness, and continuing, if narrowing, poetic productivity. His reputation peaked in the years immediately after the First World War; thereafter his critical fortunes slowly and steadily declined until such times as interest was reawakened by a significant publishing event. Stonesifer's biography of 1963 was accompanied by simultaneous publication of a new *Complete Poems* from Cape and a re-evaluation of Davies's whole career. Similarly in 1980, when *Young Emma* at last appeared, Davies's life and writing were re-examined in a new light. And most recently, the *Selected Poems* from Oxford University Press in 1985 not only made Davies easily accessible again to the general reader but conferred on his writing the authority of this academic press. In the 1920s, however, Davies's reputation began to sink. Archibald Macleish found himself in 1924 having to review four books of poetry by Davies, de la Mare, H.D., and Edith Sitwell in one batch, and was struck by their odd diversity. What he recognised in Davies was a poet 'capable of experience' who could 'think sensuously' and who filled his poems 'with things seen', giving as an example lines from 'The Rainbow' from *Secrets* (1924):

> The bird, that shakes a cold, wet wing,
> Chatters with ecstasy. (10)

Macleish's considered judgements on Davies's poetry were as penetrating as Edward Thomas's twenty years earlier. He observed wrily that Davies had 'changed as little as his public have wanted him to change', and then pondered the 'curious phenomenon' of 'British Nature poetry' which in 1924 seemed to have 'never gotten over Wordsworth'. Nature for these latter-day Wordsworthians is 'an idea evoked by a tree, a rainbow, a flower'; and continued, 'She [Nature] is, in other words, so different from the universe which the modern imagination conceives that she has for us no reality' (589). The cool judiciousness of this gives it an authority lacking in some English denunciations of Georgianism. Macleish recognised Davies's poetic virtues at the same time as being well aware of his limitations, and the anachronism of his poetry that could only increase as the years went by. But he also knew that Davies had a real poetic talent and a loyal following that continued to appreciate it. It was the fate of Davies's poetry during his lifetime first to achieve fame as part of the prestigious but brief Georgian movement, then to dwindle into being old-fashioned and insignificant, though persistently popular, poetry. While his writing stayed the same, the literary culture around him changed and shifted. Davies himself seemed content to present himself as merely a nature poet, as 'Evil' from *Secrets* clearly shows:

> Call me a Nature poet, nothing more,
>   Who writes of simple things, not human evil;
> And hear my grief when I confess that friends
>   Have tried their best to make a cunning devil! (*S* 48)

The label of 'Nature poet' discounts the range of Davies's writing, in both poetry and prose, over his career, its subtlety and complexity, and its engagement with evil too.

Even Davies's most loyal supporters have to recognise in the poetry he wrote after his marriage its narrowing range in depicting 'domestic and rural commonplaces' (*ST* 37). Davies does not lose his sense of social injustice but it is expressed, guiltily, from the comfort of his own home, as in 'The Two Heavens', also from *Secrets*, in which a man looks at the night sky from his house but then remembers the homeless:

> And, like a man that's guilty of a sin,
> I close my blinds, and draw my body in.
> Still thinking of that Heaven, I dare not take
> Another look, because of that man's sake;
> Who in the darkness, with his mournful eyes
> Has made *my* lighted home his paradise. (*S* 38)

The poor, among whom he numbered himself for many years, figure in his later poetry from a distance. 'The Poor', from the 1932 volume *Poems 1930-31*, begins ironically –

> Give them your silver, let the poor
>   Put on a braver show;
> Let not their cold and sullen looks
>   Depress the world with woe.

– though it ends sentimentally by celebrating the poor 'who laugh and sing' as 'Worth twice their weight in gold' (*P 1930-31* 23). Davies was still aware of social injustice, but his social position changed to a remote and rather guilty security. In 'Song of the Miners' from *The Birth of Song* of 1936, a year of high unemployment and social distress, his dormant social anger finds powerful expression:

> When starving cattle see
> Their blades of grass
> Locked up in ice that cuts
> Their mouths, like glass –
> What can they do but lie in heaps and die?

And shall our people starve,
Like these wild herds?
We, with our power to think,
Our gift of words –
Shall we lie down like these dumb brutes and die? (*BS* 26)

This is not the poet's own voice but rather the miners' collective voice, expressed in song, defying their suffering and expressing their humanity in a refusal to die passively like cattle. It is an impassioned observation of the poor, not a participation in their plight, for the phrase 'our people' is sung by the miners and does not include the poet.

Davies can also still surprise, however, by a phrase that captures a striking sensual perception, though it must be said that what's perceived tends to become tinier. In 'The River Severn', a poem from *My Garden*, an image from industrial south Wales unexpectedly appears in the lines 'My lovely Severn shines as bright / As any moon on trucks of coal' (*MG*). Technically, Davies writes in the 1920s and 30s within a limited range of poetic forms that serve his purposes well: the four-line, four-stress ballad stanza; effective use of half-rhymes ('For Sale', *A*; 'The Ghost', *LP*); and six-line stanzas ('Beauty and Brain', *LP*; 'A Cat's Example' *LM*). His old power to astonish by a shocking directness of thought or language can still occasionally reappear even at the end of his writing career. 'Competitors' from *Love Poems* of 1935 is about the conflict of friendship between men and sexual love for a woman:

I had a friend to smoke and drink,
We dined at clubs and saw the Play;
Till Love came, like the smallest wind,
And looked him quietly away.

So Friendship goes, and Love remains,
And who can question which is best –
A Friendship reared on the bottle, or
A Love that's reared at the breast? (*LP* 33)

Memories, as well as responses to nature, figure largely in the poetry of the last fifteen years of Davies's life. In 1925 Davies published *Later Days*, a sequence of memoirs of his life in London in the years before and during the war. Although the book was begun in November 1924, immediately after *Young Emma*, it has none of that book's stylistic intensity. In fact, it is written in a deliberately flat, disingenuous style under cover of which Davies gets his own back on his enemies and praises his friends. But the book is merely episodic, without a climax of self-transformation that both the earlier autobiographies have. Walter de la Mare, one of Davies's *bete noires*, is craftily shown up as snobbish when Davies recalls being asked by him how he wrote his poems, and, when he answered that he just wrote when an idea came to him, de la Mare at once replied, 'What do you mean by "an idea comes to you"?'. Davies gets the last word in his book even if not in conversation, for he writes, 'The reader will understand my confusion in trying to explain a thing that was so obvious' (*LD* 28). John Masefield fares even worse when he is praised for writing some of the 'best bad verses' in English literature. Davies adds with a straight face, 'Time after time have I tried to match those verses with lines of my own, and still I fail' (*LD* 58). In the nicest possible way Davies lets us see that the shrewd working-class man has his own critical view of those by whom he is patronised as his social and cultural betters. When he recalls the wartime dinner parties followed by poetry readings in aristocratic houses, it is clear that he was well aware of being patronised, for eventually he came to realise that he was being 'used as a public entertainer' (*LD* 137). This kind of comment shows that Osbert Sitwell was mistaken when he wrote about Davies in his memoirs, *Noble Essences* (1950), that Davies's birth and career had 'rendered him independent of class-feeling and nearly blind' to signs of it. On the contrary, Davies was perfectly aware of class feelings but his noble response was to behave towards others as if it did not exist. Only in certain poems, and particularly in *Later Days*, does he allow himself a quiet revenge against those who have put him down.

Later Days is valuable as a record of Davies's dealings with artists as well as writers, and his accounts of John, Sickert, Epstein, Rothenstein, Nicholson, and Gilman are unclouded by the rivalry that Davies felt for his fellow writers. The poet Ralph Hodgson is an exception to this, however, and he, along with his bull terrier who accompanied his master everywhere, including West End restaurants, is remembered affectionately for his love of boxing and strong tobacco. Davies commemorates the dog in jaunty doggerel that imitates Robert Burns:

> Still do I claim no man can reach
>   His highest soul's perfection,
> Until his life, from day to day,
>   *Deserves* a dog's affection.   (*LD* 73)

Hodgson even knew Davies well enough to challenge the racial prejudice that Davies says he 'had brought with [him] from America', by arguing for 'fair play' for all people. Davies says he was astonished, and counters Hodgson's idea by claiming that Hodgson is prejudiced in favour of 'coloured people, which is 'much worse'. This revealing episode ends with the two men recognising that 'this was a dangerous subject' and changing it immediately. Davies attributes his racial prejudice to his American experience rather than something he acquired in Newport, but it was a phobia he did not dispel despite mixing with London friends like Hodgson with liberal views. This ugly episode left an impression on Davies, and it is the memorability of this and other incidents that unites the scattered episodes of the book. It is Davies's sensitivity to people and events round him that gives the book its interest and value. The effects of the first world war on civilian life return to his pages, written six years later, with remarkable force and precision. He remembers seeing every soldier who was walking with a girl as a 'dead lover, with a happy and unsuspecting girl at his side' (*LD* 126); and hearing his housekeeper burst into his room one day with the words 'The birds are here'; and, 'looking out of my window, saw a number of the enemy's aeroplanes' in broad daylight (*LD* 213-4). The last chapters, however, are inscrutable and anticlimactic, for they tell in bowdlerised form the story of meeting Helen Payne who in this version is merely a housekeeper.

The last chapters of *Later Days* quarry the unpublished and unpublishable material of *Young Emma*, repeating some episodes word for word, but concealing the nature of the relationship between Davies and Payne; and without the narrative of desire and fear, the incidents don't make much sense. *The Adventures of Johnny*

Walker, Tramp (1926) also pillaged earlier books, *Beggars* and *The True Traveller*, and strung together some of their stories, though not their sexual ones, to produce the weakest of Davies's tramp books. This was a vein that had served him well but was now exhausted. Undaunted, Davies turned a second time to writing a novel which turned out to be no more successful than his first. *Dancing Mad* (1927), despite its modish twenties title, turned once again to Davies's American experience to tell the story of Norman, a painter compelled to leave a wife addicted to dancing. He becomes a tramp in the States, then lives in a London doss-house, and ends by dying in the first world war. The novel 'seems intended to preach the moral that genius will die unless it is nourished by a loving wife' (*PW* 42). The best parts of the novel are based on Davies's experiences on the Mississippi and in St Louis, probably in 1895 or 1896, and the Chicago canal. Among the least successful are the accounts of wartime Cafe Royal society as 'a place of sin'. The novel has been judged to be one of Davies's 'least wise writing ventures' (*WHDB* 127); but he felt compelled to turn his hand to any possible literary form in order to sustain his income which he felt to be all the more important with a wife to support.

Despite these anxieties, his reputation was sufficient to survive the knocks of ill-judged literary ventures. In 1926 he was awarded an honorary D.Litt by the University of Wales, which was conferred at a University Congregation in Cardiff in July 1929. The address was made by Professor W.D. Thomas of the English department at Swansea, who presented Davies to the Vice-Chancellor as 'a Welshman, a poet of distinction and a man in whose work much of the peculiarly Welsh attitude to life is expressed with singular grace and sincerity'. The professor is rather vague as to what this Welsh attitude might be except in his final sentence where he speaks of 'a people that loves beauty and homeliness' and Davies as the poet who has 'interpreted its spirit to the wider world and has revealed it to itself' (*WHDB* 150). Further honours from his countrymen came in 1930 when Newport held a civic lunch to celebrate his achievements, which he attended along with his wife on one of her very rare visits to Wales, though she did not meet members of Davies's family. Among the guests at the lunch was his old headmaster

William Richards, and the mayor with whom he insisted on having a drink before lunch at his childhood home, the Church House Inn. But not all connections with Wales were pleasant, for around this time a quarrel broke out between Davies and his half-sister Alice after the agent who collected the rents of their grandmother's cottages absconded with the accumulated rents that Davies had neglected to collect. When Davies went to Newport he visited Alice but they quarrelled bitterly and she reportedly 'yelped' at him from her door. Davies was to regret that he had allowed a situation to develop that tempted the agent, but he and Alice settled their quarrel, and Davies was able to carry on making occasional visits to see Alice and her husband and children (*ST* 37).

Davies's restlessness manifested itself in frequent moves of house. From East Grinstead the couple moved first to Sevenoaks then to Oxted, and then finally in 1931 to the village of Nailsworth in Gloucestershire in the borderlands of Wales and England. In 1930, perhaps in the afterglow of Newport's civic lunch, he had gone house-hunting around Abergavenny but found nothing to please him. In Nailsworth the Severn and Wales could be sighted from the ridge running a few miles outside the village. He visited Newport occasionally to collect his rents, go to rugby matches, and visit his half-sister and her children. Family ties were tenuous but strong. When one of Davies's nephews, the son of his sister Matilda, visited from Canada, he travelled to Nailsworth to see his uncle and aunt. As far as his home town and family were concerned Davies was happy to visit them from time to time but to maintain his essential independence from any demands they might make of him. A friend of Davies's reported his saying that he chose Nailsworth because 'he was near to Wales but not in Wales, as he wanted freedom and not to be haunted by any sort of trail from his past' (*WHDB* 150). In Nailsworth he did occasionally see the painter William Rothenstein who now lived nearby; and the Sitwells who also saw him infrequently when they were visiting Mrs Gordon Woodhouse, the harpsichord player. Osbert Sitwell recalled such visits, in his Introduction to the 1963 *Collected Poems*:

> On these occasions ... [Mrs Woodhouse] would always arrange for the Davieses to come to dinner. He would talk as if we had

met every day, asking after old friends, telling us of Jim, his pet
toad whom he fed regularly with saucers of milk – and whom,
according to Mrs. Davies, he 'encouraged' – of what he had been
writing, and of the trials to which he had been subjected by the
cruel overcharging of unworthy members of the medical profes-
sion in the neighbourhood.

'Of course, I *can* pay,' I remember his saying, *apropos* of this.
'But it will spoil my Christmas.' (xxxiii)

Jim the toad had Betty the sealyham and Pharaoh the half-blind cat
for company in the Davies household. Another human friend, Brian
Waters, walked with Davies in the Somerset moors and the towns
along the Bristol channel. Waters recalled a visit he and Davies
made to an old, low-ceilinged Somerset cider house to enjoy the
pure fermented apple-juice, and to Shapwick where Davies's oldest
friend from Sevenoaks days, the Reverend Charles Seamur, was
vicar (*BC* 14-5). Davies and his wife moved three times in
Nailsworth to houses all within a few hundred metres of each other,
but all with fine gardens that grew quite wild which they both
enjoyed. When they moved to Nailsworth Davies was fifty-eight
and ready to enjoy a quiet semi-retirement.

Davies did not give up his 'greatest joy in life', as he called his
writing (*YE* 73). In the 1930s he published five collections of new
poetry, two collections of poems, two prose books with poems (*My
Birds, My Garden*), an essay on the Cotswolds (actually on the travellers he had met there), and several fine editions of single poems or
small collections, such as *The Lover's Song-Book* produced by the
Gregynog Press in an edition of 250 copies. These expensive editions
show how Davies had become a writer appreciated by bourgeois
book-collectors, readers very different from the impoverished
working-class reader he had once been, making do with cheap editions of classic writers.

With Jonathan Cape's skillful marketing, the sales of Davies's
books stayed healthy, though by the 1930s his poetry had settled
into a familiar Georgian formula. His verse was accessible and
popular, and although it had shrunk in scope it always rested on
real responses; and this saved him from the general damnation of
the Georgian poets. He managed to remain visible to his loyal readership by continuously publishing and, in 1939, by making three

broadcasts for the BBC from Birmingham, reading his own work with skills he had learned in the salons of wartime London. His voice, which Edward Thomas was so struck by on first meeting him, and Ezra Pound too when he heard Davies reading, was 'slow and gentle' in conversation, always 'anxious to find the precise words for his meaning' (*CE* 89), and resonant with the accent of Newport. Davies was proud of his voice.

In spring 1938 he suffered a stroke in the hall of Yewdales, the house where he had moved in 1936. In September that year he attended in Newport the unveiling of a plaque on the Church House Inn commemorating his birthplace: 'Wm. Henry Davies / poet & author / born here / 1871'. The city council got the date right but the place of birth wrong. Davies seems not to have minded. It was John Masefield, the poet laureate whom Davies disliked and had mocked in *Later Days*, who gave the address at what was to be Davies's last public appearance. Davies was unwell, but responded with the laconic sentence: 'These things are usually done for people dead a hundred years or more, and so I stand a living witness to my own glorification'. He asked to be driven to Ridgeway to look at Alltyryn, and then the amphitheatre at Caerleon. Then he retired to Nailsworth, to 'Glendower' where he had moved earlier that year, and the fourth house he had lived in in the town. His health began to deteriorate in the spring of 1939, and he suffered a series of heart attacks that year. His doctors told him his heart had been weakened by the weight of his wooden leg. He sensed the approach of death and faced it with characteristic directness. The last volume of poems, *The Loneliest Mountain*, published in 1939, contains a note from the author saying that his doctor advised that the only way of prolonging his life was 'to become lazy and selfish' but whatever happened, 'the present book ends my career as a living author'. Davies died on 26 September 1940, aged sixty-nine, six months after Cape had published *The Poems of W. H. Davies*, containing 533 poems and a frontispiece portrait by Laura Knight. The funeral service was taken by the Reverend Charles Seamur, the old friend whom Davies had first met as a curate in Sevenoaks. To his friend Brian Waters he had said a few months before he died that he had done what he set out to do.

Davies's poems continued to have an active publishing life. A selection of poems, *Common Joys*, appeared in 1941, and a second impression of *Collected Poems* two years later. A selection of prose and poetry was edited by Brian Waters as *The Essential W.H. Davies* in 1951; and twelve years later the definitive biography by Stonesifer was published by Cape simultaneously with *The Complete Poems of W.H. Davies*. But Davies's complete works, prose as well as poetry, did not finally become available until after the death of Helen Davies in 1979. In the following year *Young Emma*, one of Davies's best books, at last reached the public. It was only then that all of Davies's work, with its constant intermingling of the personal and the literary, could be seen and judged for the first time.

Afterword

Two moments in Davies's life – or possibly two apocryphal stories – seem particularly revealing of him as a writer and a person. The first is during his first voyage to the United States in 1893 when, while still on board ship and yet to arrive in New York, he wrote a letter home about his arrival and landing in the city. This suggests qualities that were to shape the writer, his egotism – he is best able to imagine something if it is centred on himself – and his fantasy – he is good at telling stories, whether true or false. The second is his being spotted singing hymns in the London streets to scrape together a little money to live on, a moment that demonstrates his will to survive, his capacity for self-humiliation and his courage.

Davies's writing has frequently been called 'simple', but the term is double-edged, and brings to the fore the question of class. For certain of Davies's detractors, middle-class defenders of elite culture such as Frost and de la Mare, 'simple' suggests simple-minded, culturally naive, even crude. For those who admired his poetry, like Thomas and Pound, 'simple' signifies the direct feeling and authentic responses of a man in touch with the realities of life, and a literary technique that uses limited means to achieve subtle effects. However, the view of Davies as an accomplished literary artist in poetry and prose can hardly be sustained for all his writing. Some projects, like the novels, are misconceived. In his poetry he sometimes abandons 'simplicity' for poeticising, as in 'The Kingfisher', or for quasi-philosophising in his early, long poems, or, apparently inadvertently, is banal or awkward. This would support Davies's detractors' view of him as an incompetent who occasionally strikes lucky with an odd phrase, and whose reputation rests on his life as a tramp. But though Davies's writing is indeed sometimes technically weak or trite, often, particularly in his most original early writing, what may appear to be crudities or naiveties are really calculated effects. Davies's apparently

154

ingenuous storytelling in the prose works, or, in the poetry, his rhythmic irregularities, odd phrasing, or unexpected turns of thought, can be seen as a set of literary tactics that spring from his social position. In writing 'simply' Davies is seeking to give voice to an outsider's point of view of things, and to sidestep the demands of middle-class taste. The stylistic influence here might be modernism's, but is more likely Thomas Hardy's, for Hardy fashioned poems with their own 'cunning irregularities', as he called them in the preface to *Wessex Poems* of 1898. Davies's 'The Sleepers' from *Songs of Joy* (1911) uses rhythmic irregularity (in the first line), harsh, vivid imagery, subtle assonance (dark / car) and unexpressive tone to achieve its distinctive effects. Writing like this is risky because it leaves the writer open to the charge of incompetence:

> Ten cars rushed down the waterside
>   Like lighted coffins in the dark;
> With twenty dead men in each car,
>   That must be brought alive by work. (*SJ* 85)

Even more risky is the flat tone used to point the moral of the poem, 'These people work too hard, thought I, / And long before their time they die'. 'Simplicity' here is, paradoxically, a matter of art rather than accident. The same might be said of Davies's best prose autobiographies, the *Autobiography*, *Young Emma* and *The True Traveller*, which use considerable, but downplayed, narrative skill to present ways of life beyond the bounds of middle-class *mores*. Davies's testing task as a prose writer was to persuade readers unused to frankness about low-life or sexual life, and whose reading habits had been formed by codes of respectability and silence, to a different point of view of what it was like to be a tramp, or to go through an extraordinary love affair. Davies's absence of moral commentary, his apparent naivety about the events he narrates, what Shaw calls 'the extraordinary quietness of his narrative' (*AST* 10), are tactical devices to leave the full implications of the life-stories to the reader's imaginative projections and moral sensitivity. His silences neutralise and disarm the condemnation that conventional morality would call up, and allow surprising, unconventional responses to appear. Davies's technique here, as in his poetry, is so unobtrusive as to risk being labelled simply naive, but for the young writer especially this was an important aspect of his art.

Much of the disdain directed at Davies flowed from snobbery at his working-class Welsh origins, something Davies was well aware of. In an article of 1923, 'What I Gained and Lost By Not Staying at School', he praised Robert Burns, the inspirer of his own poetic vocation (or so he claimed), for his 'startling candour and native passion' which education would have replaced with 'we don't know what strange qualities'. Aligning himself with what he imagined as Burns' unlettered genius, Davies declares that 'although education invariably helps talent, yet a child of genius is better without it'. While this idea may have served to defend Davies against his educated, middle-class critics, it also locked him into a constricting, romantic notion of the artist as untutored genius, and came to fix his own self-image, especially in his later years. 'Leisure' is the poem by which Davies has become best known, from the 1911 volume, *Songs of Joy*, that begins, 'What is this life if, full of care, / We have no time to stand and stare'. Clichéd as it is from frequent reprinting in anthologies and readings on radio, it exemplifies the limitations of the romantic attitude, familiar since at least Wordsworth's time, of a male poet writing about his relation with nature. But all the poet is able to do in this poem is 'stand and stare' in the face of nature that has no apparent relation to the human. By the time Davies came to write this poem in 1911 the romantic attitude was exhausted. He, however, was too honest a writer to pretend to feelings about nature that he did not have. He confined himself, as Charles Williams observed in 1930, only with the effect that nature produced 'on his eyes'; necessarily a superficial effect, and so all he could do was express a 'never-ending amazement' at natural objects (73-4). His nature poetry represents a last gasp of the romantic tradition. What a re-reading of Davies now shows is that his reputation has been ill-served by the label 'nature poet' and does scant justice to his range and originality.

As a writer, Davies had several strokes of luck. He won the support of Edward Thomas in the crucial first stages of his career, then he found himself becoming one of the Georgian poets and being buoyed along by the volumes that appeared between 1912 and 1922. Although he never led this movement he somehow came to define it. By 1922 he had established a reputation and a loyal readership which kept on buying his books. When he published his first book of poetry in 1905 he was lucky to be publicised as a tramp poet at a moment when various sorts of working-class poets were fashionable. At the same time the cult of rural England was at its height, involving images of the southern English countryside existing in happy feudal slumber, so that when his *Autobiography of a Super-Tramp* was published in 1908 it slotted easily into this myth as well as being a continuation of the tramp story. Despite being mostly set in the USA, and its writer being a Welshman, the book's hero could stand as an exponent of the free life that English writers like de la Mare, Kipling, Jefferies, in their different ways, were pursuing through the myth of 'England'. In the Edwardian period Davies's autobiography was, according to John Lucas, 'bound to become popular with an audience that was typically fettered by city ways' and looking for a 'compensatory dream of the free life' (59-60). Davies's good fortune in writing a popular book about tramping, however, did not draw him into the ideology of the cult of England. He maintained his independence from that, as from so many other things; so that when the first world war arrived, it was greatly to his credit that he was not among the poetic voices rising in strident defence of the idea of England they had been nursing for years. Davies's Welshness was no doubt one reason for the distance he maintained.

That Welshness was a complex thing. Helen Thomas declared him to be 'a Welshman through and through' because he was so 'shrewd in his sizing up of people's attitudes to him' (*TA* 90), but that shrewdness owed as much to class as to nationality. His mother's side of the family was Welsh and his father's English, and in any case he lived in a city that looked outwards to both England and the world. He felt an outsider when he travelled in Welsh-speaking parts of the country, and he was treated as English by the locals. It is possible that his poetry may have been influenced indirectly by the reading of Welsh poetry in translation that one of his teachers encouraged. Part of Davies's Welshness was tied in with his family whose vicissitudes made it impossible for him, after his return from the United States, to create a traditional social role for himself in Newport. He was changed by his time in the States, and came to realise that he would have to find a way of life not shaped by conventional expectations. Davies never lived an orthodox life. After his unusual marriage to Helen Payne he chose eventually to live near but not in Wales, able to visit when he chose but also to keep his distance.

But the impetus for Davies to become a writer was the trauma of having his leg amputated, something that he did not ever write about and yet was a transforming event in his life. In the series of self-transformations that Davies effected upon himself, the struggle to become a writer after the physical and psychological suffering of amputation was no doubt the most difficult, extreme and unlikely. Brian Waters remarked that Davies mentioned his leg only once in the years he knew him, when he said that he could not walk on the grass. That proud, stoical silence defended an area of himself that was so private it never found its way into his writing, except perhaps negatively in his responsiveness to the physical lightness and freedom of birds and insects in flight. Helen Thomas believed that 'the nightmare occurrence which Davies dreaded above all others' was 'intrusion into his privacy'.

Davies's strong personality and fiercely-guarded independence made him his own man. He was in many respects an outsider not just from the respectable literary and upper-class circles he moved in during the first war, but from working-class culture too, for his particular knowledge was of the sub-cultures of the destitute and socially marginal. Davies's modest claim to fame rests on a handful of poems written in the Georgian style, along with his three original prose autobiographies, all written in the early part of his career. The best of Davies's writing has the qualities of shrewd observation and a lucid detachment, but above all, as John Lucas observed, it projects a vision of freedom that is genuine.

Select Bibliography

Books and articles by W.H. Davies referred to (arranged chronologically)

SD *The Soul's Destroyer* (Of the Author) 1905

NewP *New Poems* (Elkin Matthews) 1907

AST *The Autobiography of a Super-Tramp* [first published Fifield 1908] (OUP) 1980

NatP *Nature Poems* (Fifield) 1908

'How it Feels to be Out of Work' *English Review 1* (December 1908) 168 -171

B *Beggars* (Duckworth) 1909

FP *Farewell to Poesy* (Fifield) 1910

SJ *Songs of Joy* (Fifield) 1911

TT *The True Traveller* (Duckworth) 1912

F *Foliage: Various Poems* (Elkin Matthews) 1913

BP *The Bird of Paradise* (Methuen) 1914

CL *Child Lovers* (Fifield) 1916

PP *A Poet's Pilgrimage* (Melrose) 1918

FNP *Forty New Poems* (Fifield) 1918

SL *The Song of Life* (Fifield) 1920

HM *The Hour of Magic* (Cape) 1922

TO *True Travellers: A Tramp's Opera* (Cape) 1923

'What I Gained and Lost By Not Staying At School' *Teachers World* 29 (13 June 1923) 543

S *Secrets* (Cape) 1924

LD *Later Days* (Cape) 1925

A *Ambition and Other Poems* (Cape) 1929

P 1930-31 *Poems 1930-31* (Cape)

LP *Love Poems* (Cape) 1935

MG *My Garden* (Cape) 1933

BS *The Birth of Song* (Cape) 1936

LM *The Loneliest Mountain* (Cape) 1939

YE *Young Emma* (Cape) 1980

Other books and articles referred to (alphabetically by abbreviations)

AS William Cooke 'Alms and the Supertramp: Nineteen Unpublished Letters from W.H. Davies to Edward Thomas' *Anglo-Welsh Review* 70 (1982) 34 - 59

BC Brian Waters *The Bristol Channel* (Dent) 1955

CE Thomas Burke *City of Encounters: A London Divertissement* (Constable) 1932

CM Laura Knight 'W.H. Davies' *Cornhill Magazine* (Winter 1964-5) 282 - 92

CS Anthony Conran *The Cost of Strangeness: Essays on the English Poets of Wales* (Gomer Press) 1982

ETP R. George Thomas *Edward Thomas: A Portrait* (Clarendon Press) 1985

EWHD *The Essential W.H. Davies* Selected with an Introduction by Brian Waters (Cape) 1951

FLL William H. Pritchard *Frost: A Literary Life Reconsidered* (OUP) 1984

GMGS A. St.John Adcock *Gods of Modern Grub Street: Impressions of Contemporary Authors* (Sampson Low, Marston) 1923

GP *Georgian Poetry 1911-1922* ed. Timothy Rogers [The Critical Heritage] (Routledge and Kegan Paul) 1977

GR Robert Ross *The Georgian Revolt: Rise and Fall of a Poetic Ideal 1910-1922* (Faber) 1967

HMW Philip Jenkins *A History of Modern Wales: 1536-1990* (Longman) 1992

MEP John Rothenstein *Modern English Painters: Volume 1 Sickert to Smith* [first published 1952; revised edition 1976] (Macdonald and Jane's) 1984

NE Osbert Sitwell *Noble Essences: Being a Book of Characters* (Macmillan) 1950

NP C.K Stead *The New Poetic: Yeats to Elliot* (Hutchinson) 1980

OP Laura Knight *Oil Paint and Grease Paint* [first edition 1936] (Penguin) 1941

P Ezra Pound 'William H. Davies, Poet' *Poetry* 11, 1 (1917-18) 99 - 102

PNS Edward L. Ayers *The Promise of the New South: Life after Reconstruction* (OUP) 1992

PV Walter de la Mare *Private View* (Faber and Faber) 1953

PW *Poetry Wales* 18, 2 (1983) [W.H. Davies Special Issue] Articles by Sybil Hollingdrake, Jonathan Barker, R. George Thomas, Fiona Pearson, Lawrence W. Hockey

SA Jean Starobinski 'The Style of Autobiography' in *Autobiography: Essays Theoretical and Critical* ed. James Olney (Princeton) 1980

SE Evelyn Silber *The Sculpture of Epstein with a Complete Catalogue* (Phaidon) 1986

SIKW Clifford Bax *Some I Knew Well* (Phoenix House) 1951

SP W.H. Davies *Selected Poems* Chosen by Jonathan Barker (OUP) 1985

ST Sybil Hollingdrake *The Super-Tramp: A Biography of W. H. Davies* [second edition] (Hollydragon Books) 1980

BIBLIOGRAPHY

TA Helen Thomas *Time and Again: Memoirs and Letters* ed. Myfanwy Thomas (Carcanet) 1978

WE Jane Tompkins 'West of Everything' in *Gender, Genre and Narrative Pleasure* ed. Derek Longhurst (Unwin Hyman) 1989, 10 - 30

WEW Ernest Rhys *Wales England Wed: An Autobiography* (Dent) 1940

WHD Lawrence Hockey *W.H Davies* [Writers of Wales] (University of Wales Press) 1971

WHDB Richard J. Stonesifer *W.H. Davies: A Critical Biography* (Jonathan Cape) 1963

WN Lillian Browse *William Nicholson* (Rupert Hart-Davis) 1956

WWW Gwyn A. Williams *When Was Wales?: A History of the Welsh* (Penguin) 1991

Selected books and articles (arranged by author)

Bibliography

Sylvia Harlow *W.H. Davies: A Bibliography* [Winchester Bibliographies of Twentieth-Century Writers] (St Paul's Bibliographies; Oak Knoll Books) 1993

John Harris *A Bibliographical Guide to Twenty-Four Modern Anglo-Welsh Poets* (University of Wales Press) 1994

Criticism and Context

A. St. John Adcock 'A Cripple Poet: Realistic and Whimsical Word Pictures: Curious Life History' *Daily Mail* 22 July 1905, 3

Sean Cashman *America in the Gilded Age: From the Death of Lincoln to the Rise of Theodore Roosevelt* [third edition] (New York U. P.) 1993

Caradoc Evans 'Tramp and Poet' *Western Mail* 15 January 1916, 7

Mark Evans *Portraits by Augustus John: Family, Friends and the Famous* (National Museum of Wales) 1988

Brian Finney *The Inner I: British Literary Autobiography of the Twentieth–Century* (Faber and Faber) 1985

E. J. Hobsbawm *Industry and Empire: from 1750 to the Present Day* [Pelican Economic History of Britain, vol. 3] (Penguin) 1969

Michael Holroyd *Augustus John, The New Biography* [revised edition] (Chatto and Windus) 1996

Augustus John *Autobiography* (Cape) 1975

Philip Larkin 'Freshly Scrubbed Potato' in *Required Reading: Miscellaneous Pieces 1955-1982* (Faber and Faber) 1983

W.H. DAVIES

John Lucas *Modern English Poetry From Hardy to Hughes: A Critical Survey* (Batsford) 1986

Archibald Macleish 'Four Poets' *Yale Review* 14 (1925) 587-92

Vera Oak 'W.H. Davies' Visit to Neath' *Neath Antiquarian Society Transactions* (1977) 70-72

David Perkins *A History of Modern Poetry From the 1890s to the High Modernist Mode* (Harvard University Press) 1976

John Press 'W. H. Davies' in *Reference Guide to English Literature* ed. D.L. Kirkpatrick [2nd ed.] 3 vols. (St James Press) 1991 1, 453-54

William H. Pritchard *Frost: A Literary Life Reconsidered* (OUP) 1984

William Rothenstein *Twenty-Four Portraits with Critical Appreciations by Various Hands* [2nd series] (Chatto and Windus) 1923

Edith Sitwell *Aspects of Modern Poetry* (Duckworth) 1934

Meic Stephens (ed.) *The Oxford Companion to the Literature of Wales* (OUP) 1986

J.C. Squire *Collected Parodies* (Hodder and Stoughton) 1921

Edward Thomas 'A Poet at Last' *Daily Chronicle* 21 October 1905, 3

Gwyn Thomas *A Welsh Eye* (Hutchinson) 1964

Charles Williams *Poetry at Present* (OUP) 1930

E. Rowland Williams 'The Poetry of W.H. Davies' *Welsh Outlook* [Cardiff] October 1918, 304-07

Acknowledgements

I am grateful to Middlesex University for granting me a sabbatical during which I was able to complete this book. My thanks to Jonathan Hope and Lola Young for their encouragement, to Peter Mitchell for research assistance, and particularly to Vivien Miller and Mike Walters who provided useful references and ideas.

I would like to thank Ian Evans and Susan Pugh of Newport Public Library whose expertise helped guide me through the Local Studies Collection of the Reference Library in search of W.H. Davies.

I am especially grateful to John Powell Ward, the series editor, for his patience and tact, and for the many useful suggestions, most of which I have silently adopted.

Gareth Roberts read most of the first draft of these chapters, and his comments, made with his customary generosity and wit, greatly improved the book that emerged.

Lawrence Normand

The publisher gratefully acknowledges the Estate of W.H. Davies for permission to include quotations from his works.

Series Afterword

The border country is that region between England and Wales which is upland and lowland, both and neither. Centuries ago kings and barons fought over these Marches without their national allegiance ever being settled. It is beautiful, gentle, intriguing and often surprising. It displays majestic landscapes, which show a lot, and hide some more. People now walk it, poke into its cathedrals and bookshops, and fly over or hang-glide from its mountains, yet its mystery remains.

The subjects covered in the present series seem united by a particular kind of vision. Writers as diverse as Mary Webb, Dennis Potter and Thomas Traherne, painters and composers such as David Jones and Edward Elgar, and writers on the Welsh side such as Henry Vaughan and Arthur Machen, bear one imprint of the border woods, rivers, villages and hills. This vision is set in a special light, a cloudy, golden twilight so characteristic of the region. As you approach the border you feel it. Suddenly you are in that finally elusive terrain, looking from a bare height down onto a plain, or from the lower land up to a gap in the hills, and you want to explore it, maybe not to return.

There are more earthly aspects. From England the border meant romantic escape or colonial appropriation; from Wales it was roads to London, education or employment. Boundaries are necessarily political. Much is shared, yet different languages are spoken, in more than one sense. The series authors reflect the diversity of their subjects. They are specialists or academics; critics or biographers; poets or musicians themselves; or ordinary people with however an established reputation for writing imaginatively and directly about what moves them. They are of various ages, both sexes, Welsh and English, border people themselves or from further afield.

Would the Supertramp be remembered today, if he hadn't lost a leg in his North American wanderings? Almost certainly, for his doss-house and back-street existence, his women of all classes, his poetry and prose, even if the rock band hadn't named themselves in his memory. It all contrasts rather sharply with his entirely unsentimental love of the natural scene, which his poetry embodies like crystal-clear water. Davies was never just a Georgian, and wasn't much like them, but the reputation of both continues to accrue, if remarkably, almost a century on. Davies's life began on one side of the Bristol Channel, and ended on the other, and that remarkable circular tour is described in Lawrence Normand's account with a quite extraordinary clarity.

Index

INDEX

INDEX

About the Author

Lawrence Normand is principal lecturer in English Literary Studies at Middlesex University, London, and has taught at University of Wales Lampeter. His publications include articles on twentieth-century poetry, early modern drama and witchcraft; and in collaboration with Gareth Roberts, *Witchcraft in Early Modern Scotland: James VI's 'Demonology' and The North Berwick Witches* for the University of Exeter Press's Studies in History series.

The Border Lines Series